JOURNAL OF AMERICAN INDIAN EDUCATION

Volume 58, Numbers 1 & 2
Spring & Summer 2019

The *Journal of American Indian Education* (ISSN 0021-8731) is published three times a year in spring, summer, and fall by the University of Minnesota Press, 111 Third Avenue South, Suite 290, Minneapolis, MN 55401-2520. http://www.upress.umn.edu

Postmaster: Send address changes to *JAIE*, University of Minnesota Press, 111 Third Avenue South, Suite 290, Minneapolis, MN 55401-2520.

Inquiries about manuscript submissions should be sent to jaie@asu.edu. Further information about manuscript submission is in the back of this issue and available online at https://jaie.asu.edu/content/submit-manuscript.

Address subscription orders, changes of address, and business correspondence (including requests for permission and advertising orders) to *JAIE*, University of Minnesota Press, 111 Third Avenue South, Suite 290, Minneapolis, MN 55401-2520.

Subscriptions: Regular U.S. rates: individuals, 1 year (three issues) $38; libraries, 1 year $81. Other countries add $5 for each year's subscription. Checks should be made payable to the University of Minnesota Press. Back issues published after 2014: $21.50 (plus $6 shipping for the first copy, $1.25 for each additional copy inside the United States; $9.50 shipping for the first copy, $6 for each additional copy outside the United States). Back issues published before 2015: Please contact jaie@asu.edu.

Digital institutional subscriptions to the *Journal of American Indian Education* are available online through the JSTOR Current Scholarship Program at http://www.jstor.org/r/umnpress.

Jameson D. Lopez (Quechan)
University of Arizona

Allan Luke
Queensland University of Technology

Ananda M. Marin (Choctaw descent)
University of California, Los Angeles

Nathan Martin
Arizona State University

Stephen May
University of Auckland

Douglas L. Medin
Northwestern University

Sharon Nelson-Barber
(Rappahannock)
WestEd

Sheilah E. Nicholas (Hopi)
University of Arizona

Leonie Pihama (Māori)
University of Waikato

Jon Reyhner
Northern Arizona University

Monty Roessel (Diné)
Diné College

Mary Eunice Romero-Little (Cochiti)
Arizona State University

Heather Shotton
(Wichita/Kiowa/Cheyenne)
University of Oklahoma

Graham Smith (Māori)
Te Whare Wananga o Awanuiarangi

Linda Tuhiwai Smith (Māori)
University of Waikato

Elizabeth Sumida Huaman
(Wanka/Quechua)
University of Minnesota

Malia Villegas (Alutiiq/Sugpiaq)
Afognak Native Corporation

Stephanie Waterman (Onondaga)
University of Toronto

Leisy T. Wyman
University of Arizona

VOLUME 58, NUMBERS 1 & 2, SPRING &
SUMMER 2019

JOURNAL OF AMERICAN INDIAN EDUCATION

Editors' Introduction

WE BEGIN *JAIE'S* 58TH VOLUME YEAR with a double issue that addresses Indigenous education across the lifespan. From a macro-level investigation of higher education outcomes and economic (dis)parity, to in-depth qualitative analyses of personal and school-level experiences in Canada and the United States, to a micro-level study of early childhood education, to grounded reports of university transformations "from the inside out," the articles resonate with lessons on equity, Indigenous sovereignty, and the crucial role of Indigenous educators and communities in education reform.

We introduce the issue with powerful if troubling findings from the study "Returns to Higher Education for American Indian and Alaska Native Students," by Caitlyn Keo, Amy Peterson, and Kristine West. In this article the authors tackle policymakers' assumptions that increasing higher education attainment across racial groups will eliminate post-graduation gaps in earnings, employment, and labor force participation. Using data from the American Community Survey, they focus on how earning a bachelor's degree affects labor market outcomes for different groups, paying particular attention to American Indians and Alaska Natives (AIs/ANs), whose small numbers relative to the overall population often leads to their exclusion from large quantitative studies—what Shotton, Lowe, and Waterman (2013) refer to as the asterisk effect (see also Lopez & Marley, 2018). Keo and colleagues' findings raise profound questions for AI/AN communities: AI/AN college graduates reap larger returns in terms of labor force participation and employment but experience smaller gains in earnings than otherwise similar White college graduates. The authors meticulously consider the social and historical contexts for their findings, carefully pointing out the diverse variables that the dataset does not capture, and conclude that policies promoting higher education are "necessary but not sufficient to address White-AI/AN labor market disparities." Their article presents a sophisticated and nuanced quantitative analysis in terms clear to readers who do not share the authors' grounding in economics. Their compelling evidence leads to two conclusions—one relative to subject and one to method—that are critically important to *JAIE* readers: (a) "[H]igher education may exacerbate rather than alleviate racial disparities, which is troubling both ethically and economically;" and (b) "[L]umping AIs/ANs with 'other,' as is commonly done in response to small sample sizes, is misleading and obscures important details."

From this macro-level analysis in the United States we move to the stories of Indigenous experiences with Canadian schools explored by Erica Neeganagwedgin and captured in the words of a study participant that give title to the article: "There Needs to Be Full Recognition of Who We Are Beyond Symbolic Gestures." In this study, Neeganagwedgin masterfully weaves together the history of Canadian education for Indigenous peoples with the experiences of those who lived that history, all of whom were enrolled in postsecondary education at the time of the study. Using an "Indigenous pedagogy of story-telling and knowledge-sharing," the author draws out four themes from participants' narratives: (a) the importance of and relationships to land; (b) reverberating traumas from the history of colonial schooling; (c) the all-too-common experience of being singled out as "the" Native expert when mainstream curricula turn (briefly) to Native content; and (d) the importance of centering Indigenous ways of knowing within contemporary school curricula and pedagogy. The latter practice, Neeganagwedgin argues, is essential if the goals of Canada's Truth and Reconciliation Commission are to be met. Drawing on an extensive body of Indigenous scholarship and the voices of her research participants, she calls for the "prioritization and normalization of Indigenous-focused curricula" across grade levels and throughout the Canadian education system. Notably, some education entities, such as the First Nations School of Toronto (https://schoolweb.tdsb.on.ca/FNST), are heeding this call, providing models for wider education reform. While recognizing the challenges, this article also illuminates the possibilities for positive change when Indigenous authority over Indigenous schooling is a core tenet of education policy and practice.

In "Ways of Seeing and Responding to a School in Santee Sioux Country," Aprille Phillips takes readers to the U.S. State of Nebraska, elegantly chronicling how legislatively mandated educational intervention programs systematically fail to serve Indigenous communities, schools, and students by privileging external expertise and standardized assessment measures over culturally responsive collaboration and policies. Phillips examines how state policymakers, leaders, and intermediaries like herself who implemented Legislative Bill #438 (which came to be known as AQuESTT, Accountability for a Quality Education

System Today and Tomorrow) saw, understood, and responded to school educators and community members at Santee Community Schools (SCS) on the Santee Sioux reservation. The Santee school was designated one of three "priority" schools mandated for intervention in a system the state promised would be collaborative and responsive to what the school principal called "Santee DNA," or Santee ways of knowing. As Phillips' evidence reveals, however, local educators and the community were not viewed as co-decision makers; instead, they became objects of mandates they had very little choice in developing. Sadly, the Santee school case illustrates historically entrenched patterns of assimilationist paternalism directing the course of American Indian education, even as it points toward the emancipatory possibilities of developing culturally responsive policy that attends to local context and voice, based on a clear understanding of the history and sovereignty of Indigenous peoples.

We return to the Canadian context in "Improving Kindergarten and Grade One Indigenous Students' On-Task Behavior with the Use of Movement Integration," in which Serene Kerpan, M. Louise Humbert, Carol D. Rodgers, and Alexandra L. Stoddart focus on movement integration (MI), opportunities for children's increased physical activity during classroom time. Recognizing that successful early childhood education for Indigenous children depends on integrating community-specific cultural beliefs and behaviors, the authors worked in close partnership with school administrators and parents in an on-reserve school in Canada to design a study to test if MI helped students master self-regulation. Self-regulation includes a diverse range of behaviors, such as attention and responsiveness to others; research with non-Native children demonstrates this is an important component of academic success throughout the schooling years. Since self-regulation is a Western concept, the authors relied on the perspectives of community participants, who agreed that "whether a child is learning math, science, or language from either pedagogical worldview (Indigenous or Euro-Western) they need to be able to exhibit self-regulation to learn." When the children did not receive a physical activity break in a lesson their ability to stay on task dropped significantly, while their ability to stay on-task increased from the beginning of the lesson to the end when a short physical activity break occurred in the middle of a lesson. The Editors join the authors in hoping that this study can help teachers under pressure use all available class time for learner-sensitive pedagogy. MI integrates academic content in the physical activity break; based on the considerable increase in on-task behavior after the physical activity intervention, the authors argue that taking five minutes to allow children to get active has greater academic benefit than continuing with a sedentary lesson.

We wrap up the combined issue with two Reports From the Field (RFTF) that provide analyses of innovative education models in higher education. In "Indigenous Research Perspectives in the State of New Mexico: Implications for Working with Schools and Communities," Robin Zape-tah-hol-ah Minthorn, Lorenda Belone, Glenabah Martinez, and Christine Sims—faculty members in the University of New Mexico College of Education (COE)—offer a theoretical/conceptual and descriptive portrait of educational sovereignty-in-action with regard to research with Indigenous peoples in the State of New Mexico. Recognizing that research has historically been (and continues to be) on and about rather than with and for Indigenous communities, the authors present a research framework rooted in a solid recognition of tribal sovereignty and a philosophy of "cultivating authentic relationships with Native nations" in New Mexico and beyond. The authors take a firm stand in this work, noting that as Indigenous scholars "it is our responsibility to educate and advocate for the accountability, understanding, and respect that should be afforded to each tribal community." They conclude with concrete examples of how this can be accomplished through initiatives such as university-sponsored conferences that intentionally include Native youth and communities, coursework taught by Native faculty through which all COE graduate students expand their knowledge of Indigenous community-based research, and research MOUs that engage Indigenous community stakeholders and ensure accountability and effectiveness. "Our hope," Minthorn and colleagues add, "is that these actions will encourage other institutions of higher education to follow suit."

The second report, "Pugtallgutkellriit: Developing Researcher Identities in a Participatory Action Research Collaborative," describes how two non-Native faculty at the University of Alaska Fairbanks (Sabine Siekmann and Joan Parker Webster) and four Yup'ik doctoral students with years of experience teaching in Yup'ik medium schools (Sally Angass'aq Samson, Catherine Keggutailnguq Moses, Panigkaq Agatha John-Shields, and Sheila Cingarkaq Wallace) worked together over 11 years in increasingly collaborative and productive ways. The Collaborative used and reflected on Participatory Action Research (PAR) frameworks in their individual research, mutual grant-funded research, and program evaluations. Their conversations about PAR led them to question the seemingly discrete "steps" of the research cycle, especially when action was identified as a "final" step. They productively applied the

Yup'ik concept of upterrlainarluta, "always getting ready," to the notion of action in the research cycle. After several years, they named their collaborative Pugtallgutkellriit—those who float together as one—referring to how a subsistence fishing net is held up by floats that must be on the same level, "floating together" in order to catch fish. The RFTF details how the doctoral students' complex positionalities and identities as researchers evolved through three periods: during enrollment in the master's program, while in residency at the beginning of the PhD program, and as activist teacher-researchers/PhD candidates returning to their communities. The voices and experiences of this group of intellectual sisters enrich the realm of possibilities for meaningful Indigenous engagement with, success within, and contributions to higher education institutions and graduate degree programs.

Finally, with this first issue of 2019 we welcome back long-standing editorial board members and several new board members. New board members beginning their terms in 2019 include Dr. Donna Deyhle, University of Utah, Emerita; Dr. Kaiwipuni Lipe (Native Hawaiian) and Dr. Noelani Goodyear-Ka'ōpua (Native Hawaiian), both at the University of Hawai'i at Mānoa; Dr. Jameson D. Lopez (Quechan), University of Arizona; and Dr. Leoni Pihama (Māori), University of Waikato.

We also welcome two colleagues who have graciously joined the editorial team as associate editors: Dr. Angelina E. Castagno, Professor of Educational Leadership and Foundations at Northern Arizona University, and Dr. Patricia D. Quijada Cerecer (Chicana/Cupeño), Associate Professor of Education at the University of California, Davis. Both are internationally recognized scholars of Indigenous education. Trained as an educational anthropologist, Dr. Castagno's research and teaching focus on institutions, policies, and the ways students and communities engage systems of race and power; she is especially interested in issues of whiteness and Indigenous education. Dr. Quijada Cerecer's scholarship addresses Native American and Latinx youth identity formation, transitions to college, and access and equity in Pre–K–20 education systems for students of color.

In the past few years, the editors have noticed an increase in the number of manuscripts submitted to *JAIE*, increased interdisciplinarity of scholars submitting manuscripts, and more manuscripts coming from scholars outside the United States. We see these changes as signs of the journal's robust health as we move forward into 2019. Remarkably, this will be the 60th year since the establishment of the home of the journal, the Center for Indian Education at Arizona State University. The Center's founding mission was to serve the educational and cultural needs of children in the 22 tribal nations and communities in the State of Arizona. While the Center's work has expanded beyond Arizona, it remains guided by the vision of working to assist Indigenous children and communities in creating futures of their own making.

We thank you—our readers—for your ongoing efforts to achieve this vision, and for your support of *JAIE*.

Respectfully,

Bryan McKinley Jones Brayboy, K. Tsianina Lomawaima, and *Teresa L. McCarty,* Editors
Angelina E. Castagno and *Patricia D. Quijado Cerecer,* Associate Editors

REFERENCES

Lopez, J. D., & Marley, S. C. (2018). Postsecondary research and recommendations for federal datasets with American Indians and Alaska Natives: Challenges and future directions. *Journal of American Indian Education, 57*(2), 5–34.

Shotton, H. J., Lowe, S. C., & Waterman, S. J. (Eds.) (2013). *Beyond the asterisk: Understanding Native students in higher education.* Sterling, VA: Stylus.

Returns to Higher Education for American Indian and Alaska Native Students

CAITLYN KEO, AMY PETERSON, AND KRISTINE WEST

Policies aimed at increasing higher education attainment are central to efforts to eliminate racial gaps in earnings, employment, and labor force participation. We use data from the American Community Survey spanning 2008–2016 to investigate the increases in these labor market outcomes associated with obtaining a bachelor's degree—what economists term "returns to higher education"—by racial groups with particular attention to the returns realized by American Indian and Alaska Natives (AIs/ANs). We find that AI/AN college graduates reap larger returns in terms of labor force participation and employment but experience smaller gains in earnings than otherwise similar White college graduates. These results suggest that policies promoting higher education are necessary but not sufficient to address White-AI/AN labor market disparities.

CLEAR EVIDENCE INDICATES that a bachelor's degree increases employment and earnings (e.g., Abel & Dietz, 2014; James, 2012). We estimate that, on average, a bachelor's degree or higher increases the odds of employment by 7.6 percentage points and earnings by 60 percent.[1] Economists refer to these increases as the "returns to higher education."[2] There is mixed evidence, however, on if and how the returns to higher education vary by race (Barrow & Rouse, 2005; Cooper & Cohn, 1997; Gaddis, 2014; Monks, 2000; Perna, 2005). We add to this literature and find that the returns to higher education, particularly when measured by earnings, are larger for Whites than for other racial groups. This means that higher education may exacerbate rather than alleviate racial disparities, which is troubling both ethically and economically. Ethically, higher education, especially at publicly supported institutions, should not yield systemically different results by race. Economically, disparities indicate untapped opportunities for growth, and low returns to college can dampen the incentive to pursue higher education and make it harder for non-White students to repay student loan debt. A fuller and more detailed understanding of how returns to education differ by race will improve policies intended to address these ethical and economic concerns.

Previous research on differences in the returns to higher education has focused largely on Black-White earnings and employment gaps. We extend the analysis to focus on American Indian and Alaska Natives (AIs/ANs), a group that is often lumped in with "other" when disaggregating by race. Using data from the American Community Survey (ACS) from 2008–2016 that includes detailed measures of racial identity, we pursue a simple research question: Are returns to higher education different for AIs/ANs than for other racial groups?

Notably, our empirical strategy stops short of allowing for causal identification of the returns to education because we are unable to deal with selection bias.[3] As we are interested in relative statements, we argue that our methodology is robust, conditional on the assumption that the selection bias is similar across racial groups. Rather than causal estimates, our results are descriptive. Our descriptive statistics, however, are more nuanced than simple comparisons of means because we control for observable characteristics such as age and gender to better isolate the relationship between education, racial identity, and labor market outcomes. While we can only highlight differences in the returns to higher education, not speak to why differences exist, we hope this evidence provides support and motivation for further research into both potential mechanisms and remedies.

Our finding that the returns to higher education differ for AIS/ANS and other racial groups should not be taken as evidence that higher education is not important for AI/AN students. Instead, what we show is that policies that promote higher education are necessary but not sufficient to close gaps in earnings, employment, and labor force participation. These results serve as a reminder that higher education interventions will not have their full impact unless coupled with other policies that attack the remaining sources of inequality, including the legacy of unequal family resources and systemic and institutional discrimination.[4] Researchers and practitioners who work on policies that promote higher education enrollment, persistence, and completion, or who work on issues of unemployment and underemployment, may find our results quantify what qualitative observation and anecdote have already made evident. In this case, our estimates will help them make the case for continued and increased support for their important work.

Previous Literature

Plentiful evidence describes racial gaps in higher education attendance, persistence, and completion. A large body of research describes the historic and current socioeconomic context for AI/AN students in higher education (e.g., Akee et al. 2010; Brayboy, Solyom, & Castagno, 2015; Cunningham, 2007; Feir, 2016; Musu-Gillette et al., 2017; Postsecondary National Policy Institute, 2018), as well as how family and cultural characteristics influence educational attainment (e.g., Akee & Yazzie-Mintz, 2011; Guillory & Wolverton, 2008). The Postsecondary National Policy Institute summarizes recent trends. In 2017, the higher education participation rate for Native American students fell below 20 percent and the share with at least a bachelor's degree was 16 percent—compared to 42 percent for Whites. Among American racial, ethnic, and cultural groups, AIs/ANs are distinctive for their political recognition as domestic sovereign nations. AI/AN higher education is unique, in part, because there are treaty agreements governing the federal government's responsibility toward tribal nations. As a result, the federal government helps support the network of tribal colleges and universities (TCUs) that serve predominantly AI/AN students. While it is important to interpret our findings in this larger historical and socio-economic setting, we are unable to directly address much of this crucial context because we are limited to the variables collected in the ACS. For example, we do not know which students attend TCUs.

There is also a rich body of research in economics on racial disparities in the labor market (e.g., Bertrand & Mullainathan, 2004; Carneiro and Heckman, 2005; Heckman, 1998; Hurst, 1997) as well as a long-standing and careful literature on the returns to education (e.g., Barrow & Rouse, 2005; Card & Krueger, 1992; Carneiro, Heckman, & Vytlacil, 2011; Harmon & Oosterbeek, 2003; Psacharopoulos & Patrinos, 2004). Unfortunately, more often than not in economic research, AIs/ANs are tallied in the "other" racial category due to small sample sizes, but a handful of studies focus on AI/AN outcomes, which we summarize below.

Most notably and recently, Barrow and Rouse (2005) ask whether returns to schooling differ by race and ethnicity. Using U.S. Decennial Census data they find that from 1980 to 1990 returns to education increased dramatically for all race/ethnic groups. From 1990 to 2000, however, returns to each additional year of schooling increased for Whites, African Americans, and Asian/Pacific Islanders but fell slightly for

AI/AN and Hispanic workers. They go on to examine returns in the National Longitudinal Survey of Youth 79 Cohort (NLSY79) but do not report results for AIs/ANs presumably due to small sample size. Although the authors conclude that there is little difference in the returns to schooling by race and ethnicity, they are unable to probe the returns for AIs/ANs and the suggestion of divergence in the 1990s indicates a need for more work in this area. Indeed, the authors caution that further research is needed to fully understand potential heterogeneity.

In earlier work, Kimmel (1997) compares earnings for American Indian (AI), White, and Black respondents in the 1987 National Medical Expenditures Survey with a particular emphasis on rural locations. Kimmel finds that for men, only 14 percent of the AI-White earnings gap is unexplained by observable demographic and job characteristics. For women, however, 66 percent of the AI-White earnings gap remains unexplained. Further, she concludes that in rural areas AI and White workers both experience very small returns to education relative to White workers in urban settings.[5] Also related to geographic location, Gitter & Reagan (2002) find that living on or near a reservation is negatively correlated with labor market outcomes for AI men. Among AI men, those who currently reside in a county with a reservation are 11 to 14 percentage points less likely to be employed than those who reside elsewhere. Moreover, AI men who lived in a county with a reservation at age 14 are five to ten percentage points less likely to be employed than counterparts from a nationally representative cross section of the same birth cohort.

Recent evidence indicates that AI/AN workers experience nontrivial occupational sorting, another potential mechanism to explain different labor market outcomes. Wise, Liebler, and Todd (2017) find that AI/AN workers are overrepresented in low-skill occupations and underrepresented in high-skill occupations relative to non-Hispanic White workers. Gaps in educational attainment explain some but not all of this sorting. Wise et al. (2017) find that this occupational dissimilarity is persistent across education levels and is stronger for men than women. Further they find no evidence of changes over time.

Austin (2013) investigates the employment gap between AI and White workers using data from the American Community Survey. Specifically, he measures the difference in the odds of employment conditional on demographic covariates and finds that the employment rate for prime age AI workers is 64.7 percent, a full 13.4 percentage points lower than prime age White workers. He concludes that postsecondary education is the factor most likely to increase the odds of securing employment for AI workers, finding that AI with advanced degrees (greater than a BA) are seven times as likely to be employed as AIs with less than a high school diploma. He does not, however, offer evidence on whether postsecondary education is any more or less important for AI workers than it is for White workers. He also finds that South Dakota, North Dakota, Iowa, Minnesota, Wisconsin, and Montana have the largest AI-White employment gaps and that the Tlingit-Haida (Alaska), Aleut (Alaska), Cherokee (Oklahoma), and Choctaw (Oklahoma) have significantly higher employment rates than other tribes after controlling for demographics such as gender, age, and marital status. This points to the diversity of AI experiences and possibly policy lessons from specific tribal settings.

Data and Method

To estimate returns to higher education for AIs/ANs and other racial groups, we use data from the American Community Survey (ACS) spanning 2008–2016.[6] The ACS surveys are annual weighted samples of one percent of the U.S. population. All analyses make use of the sampling weights provided, yielding a nationally representative sample. Since 2005 these surveys have offered improved options for self-identification, tribal selections, and homeland designations. These improvements enable us to provide an updated and nuanced study of the returns to education for AI/AN communities.

Our final analytic sample of prime aged adults (ages 25–55) includes approximately 210,000 respondents who identify as AI/AN and nearly 11 million non-AI/AN respondents.[7] Following Wise et al. (2017), we separate AI/AN respondents into mutually exclusive subgroups: those who identify as AI/AN only (approximately 100,000), those who identify as AI/AN and at least one other race (approximately 75,000), and those who identify as AI/AN and Hispanic (approximately 34,000).[8] Table 1 has the exact sample size for each of these subgroups and other racial/ethnic categories by level of education.[9] Table 1 shows that, among prime-aged workers, AIs/ANs complete associate degrees at similar rates to Whites and are even more likely than Whites to have some college (but no degree). In contrast, AIs/ANs lag significantly behind Whites in the Bachelor's degree or higher (BA+) category. Indeed, among all of the racial/ethnic categories the

Table 1. Education Levels by Race, Ages 25–55

	(1) Total	(2) No higher education	(3) Some college	(4) Associate degree	(5) Bachelor's degree+
White	7,412,480	2,376,342	1,620,083	740,046	2,676,009
	62.1%	32.2%	22.3%	9.8%	35.7%
AI/AN alone	100,440	51,910	27,361	8,830	12339
	0.7%	49.2%	27.9%	9.0%	14.0%
AI/AN and	75,548	28,412	22,470	7,612	17,054
other race	0.6%	36.4%	30.3%	10.3%	23.0%
AI/AN and	33,967	17,650	8,297	2,532	5,488
Hispanic	0.3%	53.8%	23.9%	7.0%	15.3%
Hispanic	1,566,165	918,934	294,196	99,723	253,312
	16.8%	61.0%	18.4%	6.1%	14.6%
Black,	1,163,097	528,532	303,647	96,882	234,036
non-Hispanic	12.5%	44.2%	27.0%	8.6%	20.3%
Asian Pacific	628,876	141,964	81,983	44,684	360,245
Islander,	5.9%	23.7%	13.3%	7.0%	56.0%
non-Hispanic					
Other race,	19,169	7,263	3,718	1,562	6,626
non-Hispanic	0.2%	39.3%	18.8%	7.9%	34.1%
Two or more	99,268	26,133	24,041	9,368	39,726
races,	0.9%	26.8%	25.0%	9.4%	38.9%
non-AI/AN					
and non-					
Hispanic					
Total	11,099,010	4,097,140	2,385,796	1,011,239	3,604,835
		38.2%	21.8%	8.8%	31.2%

Note: The percentages provided use survey weights and the observation counts are unweighted. All race categories are mutually exclusive.

Source: Authors' calculations based on ACS 2008–2016.

AI/AN-only population has the lowest percentage of workers with a BA or higher.

Our main empirical strategy is an earnings equation in the style of Mincer (Mincer, 1974; Heckman, Lochner, & Todd, 2006). Specifically, we use ordinary least squares estimates of

$$y_{its} = \alpha + \beta_j Educ_{ij} + \gamma Exp_i + \gamma Exp2_i + \delta_h Race_{ih} + \kappa_{ij} * Race_{ih}$$
$$+ \theta_k X_{ik} + \rho_t Year_{it} + t_s State_{is} + \varepsilon_{its} \qquad (1)$$

where y is a labor market outcome for person i in time t and state s. We use three different labor market outcomes: labor force participation (LFP), employment, and log earnings. Earnings are measured as total pretax wage and salary income for the year prior to the surveyed year. This includes wages, salaries, commissions, cash bonuses, tips, and other monetary income from the individual's employer. Earnings do not include income from business, farm, self-employment, social security, public assistance, or other income that has not been earned from an employer.[10]

Educ measures j categories of education beyond high school in the form of indicator variables for some college (but no degree), an associate degree, a bachelor's degree, or higher (i.e., a master's, professional, or doctoral degree).[11] *Exp* is a linear and a quadratic of potential experience (age minus years of schooling minus six) and *Race* is a vector, indexed by h, including but not limited to AI/AN alone and AI/AN in combination with another race and AI/AN in combination with Hispanic. The omitted racial category is non-Hispanic White; thus the β coefficient measures the return to a degree for White workers and the ϑ coefficients on the interaction of education and race measure the marginal return to education for each non-White group. *X* is a vector of k demographic controls listed in Table 2,[12] and ρ and τ are time (year) and state fixed effects.

This identification strategy has some limitations. It is unable to address the selection bias inherent in postsecondary educational attainment. Students decide whether or not to pursue education in part based on their own assessment of their abilities and likelihood of increased earnings and employment. Further, they pursue education knowing their own preferences about labor force participation. A large body of labor economic theory focuses on how to address this problem (e.g., Angrist & Krueger, 1999), but none are particularly well suited for our data. Instead, we use the simple cross-sectional estimates and note the caveat that the results stop short of causal identification. Importantly, our focus is not as much on the returns to postsecondary education as on the *relative* returns to postsecondary education across racial groups. The key assumption is that the selection bias works similarly for AI/AN and White students (and/or students from other racial groups). It is possible that the utility functions, the constraints, and the parameters that determine selection into postsecondary education are fundamentally different for AI/AN students than for White students.[13] Since we cannot rule out differential selection, we caution the reader against strong causal statements and encourage the reader to consider this as a rigorous descriptive analysis.

Table 2. Summary Statistics, Ages 25–55

	(1) Total	(2) AI/AN
Earnings, mean	$49,667	$37,013
Log earnings, mean	10.38	10.06
Employment rate	0.93	0.88
Labor force participation rate	0.82	0.73
AI/AN alone	0.01	0.41
AI/AN and other race	0.01	0.39
AI/AN and Hispanic	0.00	0.19
Hispanic	0.17	0.19
Black	0.12	-
Asian Pacific Islander	0.06	-
Other race	0.00	-
Two or more races, non-AI/AN	0.01	-
Some college	0.22	0.28
Associate degree	0.09	0.09
Bachelor's degree	0.31	0.18
Age	40.13	39.79
Years of school	13.47	12.79
Potential experience (Age - Yrs School - 6)	20.66	21.00
Number of children	1.05	1.03
Has children	0.53	0.50
Age of youngest if has children, mean	5.11	4.87
Female	0.50	0.51
Northeast region	0.18	0.09
Midwest region	0.21	0.17
South region	0.37	0.33
West region	0.24	0.41
Married	0.56	0.44
Household size	3.12	3.17
Full-time employee	0.68	0.58
Veteran status	0.06	0.09
Rural	0.11	0.20
PUMA includes reservation	0.15	0.41
Total Observations	11,099,010	209,955

Note: Weighted summary statistics.

Source: Authors' calculations based on ACS 2008–2016.

Lastly, the sample restrictions vary somewhat depending on the dependent variable. For all analyses we focus on prime-age adults, that is, people aged 25–55. When we use LFP as the dependent variable, this is the only sample restriction. When we use employment status as the dependent variable, the sample includes only respondents who are in the labor force and, when we use earnings as the dependent variable, the sample includes only respondents who are employed.[14] Additionally, when we look at earnings we exclude part-time workers (<35 for usual hours of work per week) but we find that including part-time workers does not substantively change our findings.[15] Lastly, we adjust earnings for inflation using the CPI. After adjusting for inflation, we use only workers who earn at least $10,000 in USD2014.[16]

Table 2 provides summary statistics for the analytic sample. The first column reports on the entire analytic sample (including AI/AN respondents) and the second column is only AI/AN respondents (including AI/AN alone, AI/AN in combination, and AI/AN and Hispanic). Looking

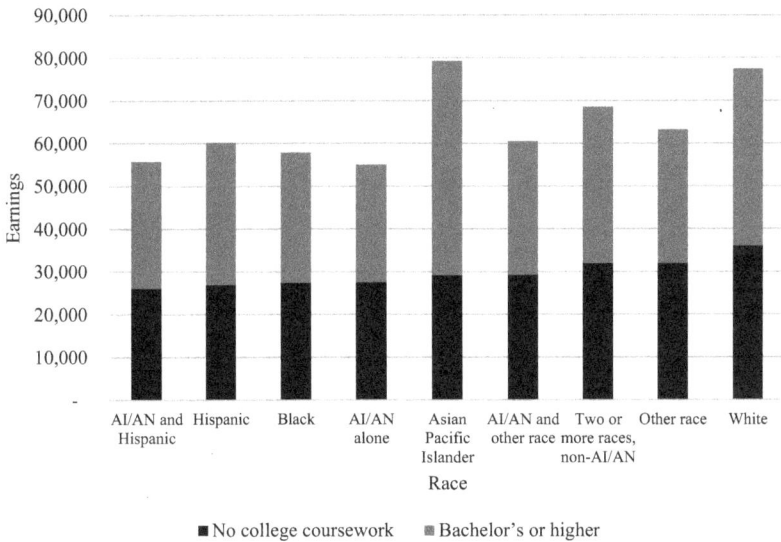

Figure 1. Earnings (US dollars) by race and education, ages 25–55.
(Note: The earnings by race and education and the percent increase in earnings between no college coursework and a BA+ can be found in appendix Table A1. Source: Authors' calculations based on ACS 2008–2016.)

first at the outcome variables, we see that AI/AN have lower LFP and employment rates than the general population. Further, average earnings are $49,667 for the entire sample (10.38 in log form) but only $37,013 for AI/AN (10.06 in log form). It is also the case that AIs/ANs differ from the general population on a range of potentially important demographic and geographic variables. For instance, among prime-age adults, AIs/ANs are less likely to be married and have children and are more likely to be military veterans. Geographically, AIs/ANs are over-represented in the West and in rural areas. Over 41 percent of the AIs/ANs in the sample live in a public-use microdata area (PUMA) that includes a reservation compared to less than 15 percent of the general population. Our preferred specification controls for these variables and thus isolates the disparities that remain after accounting for observable demographic and geographic differences.

Figure 1 illustrates a summary of earnings by race and education and provide intuition for our findings (appendix Table A1 reports the statistics used in this figure). The black portion at the base of each bar represents the average earnings for workers with no postsecondary experience. The gray portion stacked atop represents the additional

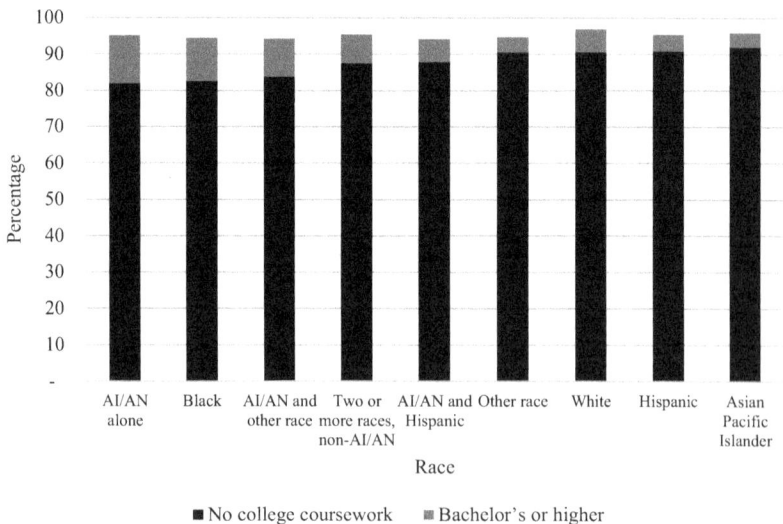

Figure 2. Employment rate (percentage) by race and education, ages 25–55. (Note: The employment rates by race and education and the percent increase in employment between no college coursework and a BA+ can be found in appendix Table A2. Source: Authors' calculations based on ACS 2008–2016.)

earnings for a worker with a BA+. The focus of this study is on the gray, i.e. the increase in earnings associated with completing higher education (BA+). Figure 1 clearly shows that there are earnings disparities for workers at all education levels and that these disparities are nuanced. The AI/AN alone category does not have the lowest earnings for workers without higher education experience but does rank lowest for workers with a BA or higher.

Similarly, Figures 2 and 3 illustrate employment and labor force participation rates by race and education (see also Tables A2 and A3 in the appendix). Among those in the labor force, AI/AN alone without any college coursework have the lowest employment rates (82 percent) of all the groups, but they experience an increase in employment by 13 percentage points with a BA+ (95 percent) (Figure 2). For White workers, 91 percent of those without college coursework are employed, which increases to 97 percent for those with a BA+. Labor force participation for those without college coursework is the lowest for AI/AN alone (62 percent), but it increases by 26 percentage points to 87 percent for those with a BA+ (Figure 3).

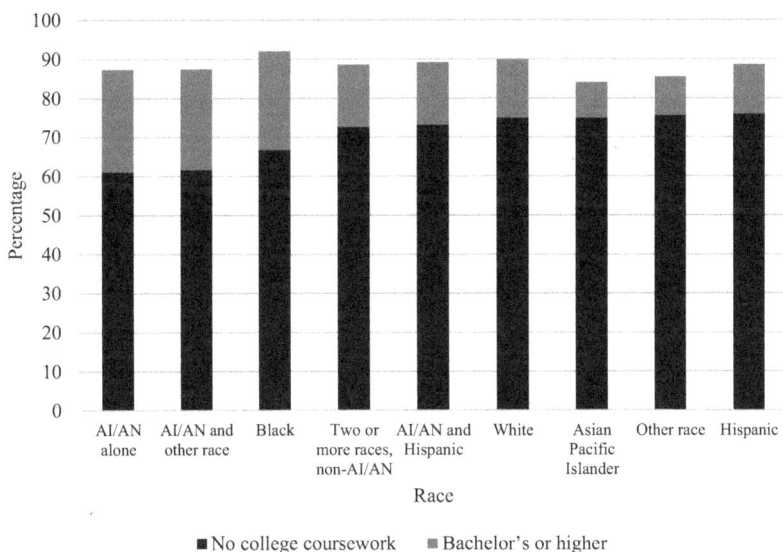

Figure 3. Labor force participation rate (percentage) by race and education, Ages 25–55. (Note: The labor force participation rates by race and education and the percent increase in LFP between no college coursework and a BA+ can be found in appendix Table A3. Source: Authors' calculations based on ACS 2008–2016.)

Results

The summary statistics in Figure 1 provide good intuition for our findings. The summary statistics, however, do not control for observable covariates such as age and geographic location. To make the analysis more robust, we turn to the econometric specification described in the methods section above. First, we report the results of our estimates of equation (1) using earnings as the dependent variable. Then we turn to employment and LFP. For each outcome we report returns to postsecondary education by race, i.e., β_j and κ_{ij}, in Table 3. In the appendix, we report separate estimates by gender.[17]

Earnings

The first column of Table 3 reports results using the natural log of earnings as the outcome variable. The coefficients, once exponated (i.e., transformed from the natural log form of earnings to its equivalent exponential form in dollars), can be interpreted as percent differences relative to the omitted category (non-Hispanic White without any college coursework). First, we affirm two well-known findings: there are large racial disparities in earnings and substantially larger earnings for workers with postsecondary education. We see this on the negative coefficients on each non-White racial group, indicating lower average

Table 3. Log Earnings, Employment Status, and Labor Force Participation, Ages 25–55

	(1) Log earnings	(2) Employment status	(3) Labor force participation
AI/AN alone	−0.063***	−0.069***	−0.069***
	[0.006]	[0.003]	[0.002]
AI/AN and other race	−0.038***	−0.050***	−0.067***
	[0.007]	[0.004]	[0.003]
AI/AN and Hispanic	−0.032***	−0.016***	−0.002
	[0.007]	[0.004]	[0.003]
Hispanic	−0.227***	0.002***	−0.001*
	[0.001]	[0.000]	[0.000]
Black	−0.128***	−0.060***	−0.031***
	[0.001]	[0.001]	[0.001]

	(1) Log earnings	(2) Employment status	(3) Labor force participation
Asian Pacific Islander	−0.224***	0.012***	0.002
	[0.002]	[0.001]	[0.001]
Other race	−0.139***	0.003	0.003
	[0.010]	[0.005]	[0.005]
Two or more races,	−0.042***	−0.018***	−0.009**
non-AI/AN	[0.006]	[0.003]	[0.003]
Some College	0.181***	0.018***	0.036***
	[0.001]	[0.000]	[0.000]
Associate degree	0.281***	0.030***	0.055***
	[0.001]	[0.000]	[0.000]
Bachelor's degree or higher	0.565***	0.037***	0.048***
	[0.001]	[0.000]	[0.000]
Potential experience	0.030***	−0.001***	0.001***
	[0.000]	[0.000]	[0.000]
Potential experience squared	−0.001***	0.000***	−0.000***
	[0.000]	[0.000]	[0.000]
AI/AN Alone * Bachelor's+	−0.080***	0.050***	0.059***
degree	[0.009]	[0.004]	[0.004]
AI/AN and other race *	−0.074***	0.033***	0.071***
Bachelor's+ degree	[0.009]	[0.004]	[0.004]
AI/AN and Hispanic *	0.078***	0.003	0.020***
Bachelor's+ degree	[0.013]	[0.005]	[0.006]
Black * Bachelor's+ degree	0.005*	0.038***	0.040***
	[0.002]	[0.001]	[0.001]
Asian * Bachelor's+ degree	0.227***	−0.019***	−0.044***
	[0.003]	[0.001]	[0.001]
Other race, non-White,	0.028	−0.014*	−0.029***
non-AI/AN * Bachelor's+ degree	[0.014]	[0.006]	[0.006]
Two or more races, non-AI/	0.010	0.010**	0.005
AN * Bachelor's+ degree	[0.007]	[0.003]	[0.003]
State Fixed Effects	Yes	Yes	Yes
Year Fixed Effects	Yes	Yes	Yes
Demographic Controls	Yes	Yes	Yes
Observations	7,096,573	8,970,289	11,099,010

Notes: Potential experience was calculated as current age minus years of school and minus six. Standard errors are reported in the brackets * $p < 0.05$
** $p < 0.01$ *** $p < 0.001$.

Source: Authors' calculations based on ACS 2008–2016.

earnings relative to Whites, and on the positive coefficients on each of the education categories, indicating higher average earnings relative to workers with no postsecondary coursework.[18]

Our main interest in this article is the differential returns to a degree. For this we turn to the coefficients on the interactions of race and education. The coefficients on these interactions reveal the marginal return for this group relative to the omitted group (White). Interacting AI/AN-alone with BA+ we find that AI/AN workers earn lower returns to postsecondary education than do their White peers. Recall that to properly interpret interaction coefficients, it is important to combine them with the main coefficient. The negative coefficient on the interaction of AI/AN-alone and BA+ does not mean that earning a BA+ is not beneficial for AI/AN workers. Instead, it means that the returns to a BA+ are strongly positive but smaller for AI/AN workers than for White workers. More specifically, a White worker with a BA+ earns on average 76 percent more than a White worker with no college coursework (exp[0.565] = 1.76, or a 76 percent difference). An AI/AN worker with a BA+ earns 64 percent more than an AI/AN worker with no college coursework (0.565 - 0.080 = 0.485; exp(0.485) = 1.64, or a 64 percent difference). The gap between AI/AN workers with no college and AI/AN workers with a BA+ is 12 percentage points narrower than the gap between White workers with no college and White workers with a BA+ (76% – 64% = 12 percentage points).[19]

Education improves earnings across all racial groups. However, on average, White workers see the largest earnings boost. AIs/ANs (and other non-White groups) see smaller gains. Given this, equalizing educational attainment alone is likely insufficient to bring AI/AN workers' earnings up to those of their White peers. Workers who identify as AI/AN-alone experience the most disadvantage; workers who identify as AI/AN in combination with another race show similar patterns but slightly smaller magnitudes. We find a similar pattern for other degree levels (not shown, full results available upon request).[20]

Employment and Labor Force Participation

In Table 3, column 2, we estimate equation (1) with employment as the dependent variable. Employment is a more basic measure of labor force success than earnings. Employment simply measures the existence of a job and does not reveal anything about the quality of employment. Some workers may be underemployed, that is, working low-wage jobs that are below their full earnings potential. Unlike earnings, employment is a binary outcome. The results presented are estimates from a linear probability model (an ordinary least squares estimate) but all results are robust to logit and/or probit specifications.

As is the case with earnings, we see clear evidence of racial disparities as well as positive returns to higher education. The coefficient on AI/AN alone indicates that AI/AN workers without any postsecondary experience have an employment rate that is 6.9 percentage points lower than the employment rate for White workers without any postsecondary experience. This is the largest racial employment gap. The gap between White and Black workers is the next largest with a 6.0 percentage point difference.[21] Higher education leads to higher odds of employment. The coefficient on BA+ indicates that White workers with at least a BA have 3.7 percentage point higher employment rates than White workers with no postsecondary experience.

Focusing on differential returns to education by race, we find that, unlike with earnings, AI/AN workers experience *larger* increases in employment associated with higher education than their White peers. There is, however, a caveat—the differential returns are not sufficient to close the employment gap. That is, the coefficient on the interaction of AI/AN-alone and a BA+ is 0.05, which is not enough to offset the coefficient on AI/AN-alone, –0.069. Taken together, AI/AN workers with a BA+ are still less likely to be employed than White workers with a BA+. Summing the coefficients reveals that employment rates for AI/AN-alone workers with a BA+ are 1.9 percentage points lower than employment rates for White workers with a BA+ (–0.069 + 0.05 = –0.019).

As was the case with earnings, AI/AN workers have lower employment rates than White workers and, while earning a bachelor's degree increases employment rates for all groups, it does so at differing rates. As is the case with earnings, the pattern is similar but the magnitudes are smaller for AI/AN workers who also identify as another race. In comparison to other racial employment gaps, the White-AI/AN pattern seems much more similar to the White-Black gap than the White-other gap. This suggests that lumping AI/AN with "other," as is commonly done in response to small sample sizes, is misleading and obscures important details.[22]

Lastly, in Table 3 column 3, we use labor force participation as our outcome. Earnings are contingent on being employed, and employment is contingent on being in the labor force. Thus, labor force participation is our broadest outcome measure. LFP measures labor supply on the extensive (decision to work) rather than the intensive (decision on how much to work) margin. As with employment and earnings, we see that across specifications, LFP rates are lower for AI/AN than for Whites. For prime age adults (25–55) without any postsecondary experience, the AI/AN population has a 6.9 percentage point lower LFP rate than the White population. Unsurprisingly, LFP increases with education and increases at a diminishing rate with experience.

When we interact race and education level, the increase in LFP associated with a BA is higher for AIs/ANs than for Whites. As was the case with employment rates, this is good news but with an important caveat. The larger increases in LFP are not sufficient to erase the base gap. For instance, AI/AN BA+ holders have a marginal increase in LFP of 5.9 percentage points, which does not make up for the 6.9 percentage point gap. Indeed, taken together, these coefficients show that AI/AN BA+ holders have 1.0 percentage point lower LFP rates than White BA+ holders ($-0.069 + 0.059 = -0.01$).[23]

In sum, when we use employment and LFP to assess the returns to postsecondary education, we find that education narrows but does not eliminate employment gaps between AIs/ANs and Whites. This more optimistic story echoes the findings in Austin (2013). We note, however, that employment and LFP may be particularly fraught with selection bias and further research is needed before strong causal claims can be made.

Discussion

We study the returns to higher education using data from the ACS spanning 2008–2016. These surveys have unprecedented detail about AI/AN self-identification, enabling us to provide a nuanced look at earnings, employment, and LFP gaps and the role that higher education may play in closing those gaps. We find that additional education increases LFP, employment, and average earnings across the board but at different rates for different racial groups. Specifically, we find that the increases in LFP and employment associated with a bachelor's degree or higher (BA+) are 5.9 and 5.0 percentage points *more* for AIs/ANs than for Whites. The earnings premium associated with a BA+, however, is 12 percentage points *lower* for AIs/ANs than for Whites. These findings have important implications. They suggest that interventions aimed at improving college attendance and completion may have larger labor force participation and employment effects but smaller earnings effects for AI/AN communities than for other groups. Policymakers should not ignore that higher education is a good investment for all but that the earnings premium is higher returns for Whites.

Equalizing educational attainment would not be sufficient to close racial employment and earnings gaps.[24] We stress that this does not mean that policies that increase higher education are not necessary or important. The unequal returns to higher education may be a concern of secondary importance. Society may be very willing to tolerate inequality in exchange for large increases in average earnings that would result from substantial gains in higher education enrollment, persistence, and attainment. Still, reducing inequality among similarly educated workers is likely an important policy goal since inequality limits intergenerational economic mobility (Corak, 2013) and because much of the growth in income inequality in the United States has been concentrated within, rather than between, education levels (Lemieux, 2006).

It is worth reiterating that our analysis is largely descriptive in nature. We are able to control for observable demographic and geographic differences that likely impact earnings, but we are unable to control for self-selection into post-secondary education. Additionally, although the ACS has rich data on racial identity, there are more limited data on the context for each student's higher education experience. For instance, we know the highest degree level, but we do not know if the person attended a public or private institution or, for AI/AN students, if they took part in the TCU system. We also do not know student GPA or courses completed and do not know what, if any wraparound supports the students received while in college. Future work should consider how these variables mediate our results. A rich body of research examines targeted programs that support AI/AN students (e.g., Brayboy, Fann, Castagno, & Solyom, 2012). Our findings support the need for these targeted programs. Clearly, getting AI/AN students to enroll in college, and even to complete BA and advanced degrees, is only part of the story.

We also do not know how the students financed their higher education. The fact that AI/AN students experience gains in earnings but those gains in earnings are smaller than those of White students suggests that AI/AN students will have a harder time paying off college debt. Heavy debt burdens negatively impact the overall financial health of households (Elliot & Nam, 2013). This will exacerbate wealth inequalities, reduce intergenerational mobility, and may rationally discourage AI/AN students from pursuing higher education. Given this, policies that aim to increase AI/AN college going and completion should also favor grant aid over loans. A related policy would be to increase loan-forgiveness for AI/AN students. Qualitative evidence suggests that AI/AN students are disproportionately motivated to complete advanced degrees because they want to help their communities rather than for purely individual gain (Brayboy et al., 2015). A loan-forgiveness program could be linked to working in a job that directly gives back to the community. Evidence that AI/AN students may be disproportionately motivated by altruistic goals points to another area for future research. We cannot rule out the possibility that AI/AN workers are choosing to take lower-paid jobs that are rewarding in other ways.

Our results do not confirm but are nonetheless consistent with the possibility of labor market discrimination, as disparities persist after a host of controls for observable demographics are included. The labor market experience for a demographically and geographically similar White worker and AI/AN worker is different even if those workers have the same degree level. This supports further research on employer-driven discrimination and/or inequities in the Pre-K–12 educational system that could leave AI/AN students disproportionately underprepared to take full advantage of the earnings boost that college offers (Fischer & Stoddard, 2013).

In conclusion, while the analysis in this study does not offer direct policy guidance, it is an important part of the overall story of the experience of AIs/ANs in higher education. This analysis sheds light on the role that education plays in addressing and/or exacerbating racial disparities in the labor market. Our findings suggest that higher education increases earnings across the board but at differential rates by race. Thus, while college going and completion are likely key to advancing the well-being of AI/AN communities, our findings imply that increased college attainment alone will not eliminate persistent racial earnings inequalities.

Caitlyn Keo is an economics research specialist at St. Catherine University, St. Paul, MN. Her primary fields of interest are development economics and the economics of education.

Amy Peterson is a student and research assistant at St. Catherine University, St. Paul, MN. Her primary fields of interest are econometrics and actuarial science.

Kristine West is associate professor of economics at St. Catherine University, St. Paul, MN. Her primary fields of interest are labor economics, program evaluation, and the economics of education.

Table A1. Earnings (US dollars) by Race and Education, Ages 25–55

	(1) No college coursework	(2) Bachelor's or higher	(3) Percent increase
White	36,071	77,417	115%
AI/AN alone	27,513	55,001	100%
AI/AN and other race	29,345	60,513	106%
AI/AN and Hispanic	26,123	55,743	113%
Black	27,384	57,856	111%
Asian Pacific Islander	29,269	79,317	171%
Other race	32,026	63,231	97%
Two or more races, non-AI/AN	32,005	68,606	114%
Hispanic	26,922	60,150	123%
Average	29,629	64,204	117%

Note: The percent increase is calculated as the (earnings of a BA+– earnings of no college coursework) / earnings of no college coursework.

Source: Authors' calculations based on ACS 2008–2016.

Table A2. Employment Rate (Percentage) by Race and Education,
Ages 25–55

	(1) No college coursework	(2) Bachelor's or higher	(3) Percent increase
White	91	97	7%
AI/AN alone	82	95	16%
AI/AN and other race	84	94	12%
AI/AN and Hispanic	88	94	7%
Black	93	94	14%
Asian Pacific Islander	92	96	4%
Other race	91	95	5%
Two or more races, non-AI/AN	88	95	9%
Hispanic	91	95	5%
Average	98	95	9%

Source: Authors' calculations based on ACS 2008–2016.

Table A3. Labor Force Participation Rate (Percentage) by Race and Education, Ages 25–55

	(1) No college coursework	(2) Bachelor's or higher	(3) Percent increase
White	75	90	20%
AI/AN alone	61	87	43%
AI/AN and other race	62	88	42%
AI/AN and Hispanic	73	89	22%
Black	67	92	38%
Asian Pacific Islander	75	84	12%
Other race	76	86	13%
Two or more races, non-AI/AN	73	89	22%
Hispanic	76	89	17%
Average	71	88	24%

Source: Authors' calculations based on ACS 2008–2016.

Table A4. Log Earnings by Sex, Ages 25–55

	(1) All	(2) Male	(3) Female
AI/AN alone	−0.063***	−0.104***	−0.004
	[0.006]	[0.007]	[0.008]
AI/AN and other race	−0.038***	−0.056***	−0.015
	[0.007]	[0.008]	[0.011]
AI/AN and Hispanic	−0.032***	−0.034***	−0.006
	[0.007]	[0.008]	[0.011]
Hispanic	−0.227***	−0.267***	−0.170***
	[0.001]	[0.001]	[0.001]
Black	−0.128***	−0.172***	−0.069***
	[0.001]	[0.002]	[0.002]
Asian Pacific Islander	−0.224***	−0.276***	−0.150***
	[0.002]	[0.003]	[0.003]
Other race	−0.139***	−0.168***	−0.090***
	[0.010]	[0.013]	[0.016]
Two or more races, non-AI/AN	−0.042***	−0.079***	0.019*
	[0.006]	[0.008]	[0.009]
Some college	0.181***	0.189***	0.176***
	[0.001]	[0.001]	[0.001]
Associate degree	0.281***	0.261***	0.310***
	[0.001]	[0.001]	[0.001]
Bachelor's degree or higher	0.565***	0.536***	0.596***
	[0.001]	[0.001]	[0.001]
Potential experience (Age - Yrs School - 6)	0.030***	0.033***	0.030***
	[0.000]	[0.000]	[0.000]
Potential experience squared	−0.001***	−0.001***	−0.001***
	[0.000]	[0.000]	[0.000]
AI/AN Alone * Bachelor's+ degree	−0.080***	−0.079***	−0.099***
	[0.009]	[0.014]	[0.012]
AI/AN and other race * Bachelor's+ degree	−0.074***	−0.076***	−0.078***
	[0.009]	[0.013]	[0.014]
AI/AN and Hispanic * Bachelor's+ degree	0.078***	0.093***	0.023
	[0.013]	[0.019]	[0.017]
Black * Bachelor's+ degree	0.005*	−0.030***	−0.004
	[0.002]	[0.003]	[0.003]
Asian * Bachelor's+ degree	0.227***	0.268***	0.167***
	[0.003]	[0.004]	[0.004]

	(1) All	(2) Male	(3) Female
Other race, non-white, non-AI/AN * Bachelor's+ degree	0.028 [0.014]	0.046* [0.020]	−0.009 [0.021]
Two or more races, non-AI/ AN * Bachelor's+ degree	0.010 [0.007]	0.020* [0.009]	−0.030** [0.010]
Midwest region	−0.257*** [0.005]	−0.255*** [0.007]	−0.251*** [0.007]
South region	0.125*** [0.005]	0.100*** [0.007]	0.145*** [0.007]
West region	−0.027*** [0.004]	−0.006 [0.006]	−0.047*** [0.006]
Married	0.135*** [0.001]	0.173*** [0.001]	0.085*** [0.001]
Household size	−0.040*** [0.000]	−0.044*** [0.000]	−0.033*** [0.000]
Number of own children in the household	0.045*** [0.000]	0.057*** [0.001]	0.018*** [0.001]
Age of youngest child	0.000*** [0.000]	0.003*** [0.000]	−0.001*** [0.000]
Full-time employee	0.606*** [0.001]	0.634*** [0.002]	0.571*** [0.001]
Veteran status	0.064*** [0.001]	0.047*** [0.001]	0.077*** [0.002]
Rural	−0.102*** [0.001]	−0.085*** [0.001]	−0.121*** [0.001]
PUMA includes reservation	−0.028*** [0.001]	−0.019*** [0.001]	−0.038*** [0.001]
State Fixed Effects	Yes	Yes	Yes
Year Fixed Effects	Yes	Yes	Yes
Observations	7,096,573	3,714,448	3,382,125

Note: Standard errors are reported in the brackets * $p < 0.05$ ** $p < 0.01$ *** $p < 0.001$.

Source: Authors' calculations based on ACS 2008–2016.

Table A5. Employment Status by Sex, Ages 25–55

	(1) All	(2) Male	(3) Female
AI/AN alone	−0.069***	−0.071***	−0.058***
	[0.003]	[0.004]	[0.004]
AI/AN and other race	−0.050***	−0.044***	−0.053***
	[0.004]	[0.005]	[0.006]
AI/AN and Hispanic	−0.016***	−0.016***	−0.016**
	[0.004]	[0.004]	[0.006]
Hispanic	0.002***	0.014***	−0.013***
	[0.000]	[0.000]	[0.001]
Black	−0.060***	−0.055***	−0.059***
	[0.001]	[0.001]	[0.001]
Asian Pacific Islander	0.012***	0.019***	0.008***
	[0.001]	[0.001]	[0.001]
Other race	0.003	0.008	−0.003
	[0.005]	[0.006]	[0.007]
Two or more races,	−0.018***	−0.009*	−0.026***
non-AI/AN	[0.003]	[0.004]	[0.005]
Some college	0.018***	0.019***	0.018***
	[0.000]	[0.000]	[0.001]
Associate degree	0.030***	0.026***	0.033***
	[0.000]	[0.001]	[0.001]
Bachelor's degree or higher	0.037***	0.034***	0.041***
	[0.000]	[0.000]	[0.000]
Potential experience	−0.001***	−0.002***	−0.001***
	[0.000]	[0.000]	[0.000]
Potential experience squared	0.000***	0.000***	0.000***
	[0.000]	[0.000]	[0.000]
AI/AN Alone * Bachelor's+	0.050***	0.058***	0.038***
degree	[0.004]	[0.006]	[0.005]
AI/AN and other race *	0.033***	0.036***	0.028***
Bachelor's+ degree	[0.004]	[0.006]	[0.006]
AI/AN and Hispanic *	0.003	0.002	0.008
Bachelor's+ degree	[0.005]	[0.008]	[0.008]
Black * Bachelor's+ degree	0.038***	0.043***	0.034***
	[0.001]	[0.001]	[0.001]
Asian * Bachelor's+ degree	−0.019***	−0.016***	−0.025***
	[0.001]	[0.002]	[0.002]

	(1) All	(2) Male	(3) Female
Other race, non-white, non-AI/AN * Bachelor's+ degree	−0.014* [0.006]	−0.014 [0.008]	−0.015 [0.009]
Two or more races, non-AI/AN * Bachelor's+ degree	0.010** [0.003]	0.005 [0.004]	0.015** [0.005]
Midwest region	0.025*** [0.002]	0.030*** [0.003]	0.020*** [0.003]
South region	−0.005* [0.002]	0.005 [0.003]	−0.014*** [0.003]
West region	0.028*** [0.002]	0.032*** [0.002]	0.024*** [0.002]
Married	0.038*** [0.000]	0.034*** [0.000]	0.033*** [0.000]
Household size	−0.010*** [0.000]	−0.011*** [0.000]	−0.007*** [0.000]
Number of own children in the household	0.010*** [0.000]	0.011*** [0.000]	0.006*** [0.000]
Age of youngest child	0.000*** [0.000]	0.000*** [0.000]	0.001*** [0.000]
Full-time employee	0.199*** [0.000]	0.270*** [0.001]	0.155*** [0.000]
Veteran status	−0.005*** [0.000]	−0.004*** [0.000]	−0.008*** [0.001]
Rural	−0.003*** [0.000]	−0.005*** [0.001]	−0.001 [0.001]
PUMA includes reservation	−0.002*** [0.000]	−0.003*** [0.000]	−0.000 [0.001]
State Fixed Effects	Yes	Yes	Yes
Year Fixed Effects	Yes	Yes	Yes
Observations	8,970,289	4,676,720	4,293,569

Notes: Analyzes on employment do not include people who are not in the labor force. Potential experience was calculated as current age minus years of school and minus six. Standard errors are reported in the brackets * p < 0.05 ** p < 0.01 *** p < 0.001.

Source: Authors' calculations based on ACS 2008–2016.

Table A6. Labor Force Participation by Sex, Ages 25–55

	(1) All	(2) Male	(3) Female
AI/AN alone	−0.069***	−0.077***	−0.062***
	[0.002]	[0.003]	[0.004]
AI/AN and other race	−0.067***	−0.077***	−0.056***
	[0.003]	[0.004]	[0.005]
AI/AN and Hispanic	−0.002	−0.010*	0.005
	[0.003]	[0.004]	[0.006]
Hispanic	−0.001*	0.011***	−0.012***
	[0.000]	[0.000]	[0.001]
Black	−0.031***	−0.068***	0.008***
	[0.001]	[0.001]	[0.001]
Asian Pacific Islander	0.002	0.011***	−0.001
	[0.001]	[0.001]	[0.002]
Other race	0.003	0.011	−0.002
	[0.005]	[0.006]	[0.008]
Two or more races,	−0.009**	−0.017***	−0.000
non-AI/AN	[0.003]	[0.004]	[0.004]
Some college	0.036***	0.024***	0.049***
	[0.000]	[0.000]	[0.001]
Associate degree	0.055***	0.031***	0.076***
	[0.000]	[0.001]	[0.001]
Bachelor's degree or higher	0.048***	0.032***	0.063***
	[0.000]	[0.000]	[0.001]
Potential experience	0.001***	−0.001***	0.003***
	[0.000]	[0.000]	[0.000]
Potential experience squared	−0.000***	−0.000***	−0.000***
	[0.000]	[0.000]	[0.000]
AI/AN Alone * Bachelor's+	0.059***	0.073***	0.043***
	[0.004]	[0.005]	[0.006]
AI/AN and other race *	0.071***	0.084***	0.055***
Bachelor's+	[0.004]	[0.005]	[0.006]
AI/AN and Hispanic *	0.020***	0.019**	0.021*
Bachelor's+	[0.006]	[0.007]	[0.009]
Black * Bachelor's+	0.040***	0.072***	−0.001
	[0.001]	[0.001]	[0.001]
Asian * Bachelor's+	−0.044***	−0.029***	−0.063***
	[0.001]	[0.002]	[0.002]

	(1) All	(2) Male	(3) Female
Other race, non-white, non-AI/AN * Bachelor's+	−0.029*** [0.006]	−0.024** [0.008]	−0.036*** [0.010]
Two or more races, non-AI/AN * Bachelor's+	0.005 [0.003]	0.016*** [0.004]	−0.010 [0.005]
Midwest region	−0.005* [0.003]	0.001 [0.003]	−0.008* [0.004]
South region	−0.026*** [0.002]	−0.001 [0.003]	−0.050*** [0.003]
West region	−0.005* [0.002]	0.009*** [0.002]	−0.016*** [0.003]
Married	−0.006*** [0.000]	0.020*** [0.000]	−0.027*** [0.000]
Household size	0.005*** [0.000]	0.012*** [0.000]	−0.003*** [0.000]
Number of own children in the household	−0.009*** [0.000]	−0.004*** [0.000]	−0.013*** [0.000]
Age of youngest child	0.002*** [0.000]	0.001*** [0.000]	0.003*** [0.000]
Full-time employee	0.492*** [0.000]	0.468*** [0.001]	0.492*** [0.000]
Veteran status	−0.015*** [0.000]	−0.011*** [0.000]	−0.022*** [0.001]
Rural	−0.021*** [0.000]	−0.033*** [0.001]	−0.008*** [0.001]
PUMA includes reservation	−0.008*** [0.000]	−0.015*** [0.000]	−0.001* [0.001]
State Fixed Effects	Yes	Yes	Yes
Year Fixed Effects	Yes	Yes	Yes
Observations	11,099,010	5,462,006	5,637,004

Notes: Potential experience was calculated as current age minus years of school and minus six. Standard errors are reported in the brackets * $p < 0.05$ ** $p < 0.01$ *** $p < 0.001$.

Source: Authors' calculations based on ACS 2008–2016.

NOTES

This research was supported by funding from the Center for Indian Country Development (CICD) at the Federal Reserve Bank of Minneapolis: https://www .minneapolisfed.org/indiancountry. We are grateful to Dick Todd for support and guidance and to Kris Shelander for excellent research assistance. We are also grateful to participants in the CICD brown bag and the National Indian Education Association annual conference for helpful feedback on an earlier draft.

1. These magnitudes are consistent with previous research.

2. This language reflects the fact that education is an investment in human capital and that investment generates returns. These returns can be monetary— the focus of this article—and/or non-monetary such as improved health outcomes. The returns can be private (accrue to the individual) like increased earnings, or public (benefit the community), for instance, increased civic participation. Scholars from a range of disciplines are interested in the value of a degree. See, for example, Mayhew et al. (2016) for an overview of this research from perspectives other than purely economic.

3. In this case, selection bias refers to the fact that students who select into higher education are likely different from students who do not select into higher education in both observable and unobservable ways. In this article, we can control for observable characteristics such as age and gender but we cannot control for unobservable characteristics such as motivation and ability.

4. For example, the differences in the returns to higher education can stem from disparities in early childhood or K–12 education. They can also be a result of labor market discrimination. While we cannot comment on exactly which complementary policies will be most effective, our findings make the case for interventions that take into consideration differing levels of preparation and different demands from work and family, for example.

5. Kimmel's estimates depend on a sample of 975 AI males (599 employed) and 1,146 AI females (550 employed). Our analysis provides updated estimates using a much larger data source. Her identification strategy is a two-step Heckman correction with household size and marital status to control for selection into work. The observable personal and job characteristics are age, education, an indicator for more than one year out of the labor force, firm size, union status, occupation, and the share of White males in the occupation.

6. The American Community Survey is an ongoing survey by the U.S. Census Bureau. We accessed the harmonized data from the Integrated Public Use Microdata Series, IPUMS (Ruggles, Genadek, Goeken, Grover, & Sobek, 2015).

7. If a person identifies as more than one group, including Hispanic, they are categorized as Hispanic. Other race, non-Hispanic is a population of people who identified as "some other race, alone or in combination." This is clearly not consistent with sociological literature that is intentional about the distinction between race and ethnicity. For simplicity, we refer to race and ethnicity as race throughout.

8. As the results will make clear, we see evidence that AI/AN-Hispanic experience very different labor market outcomes. In the current study we focus our discussion on results for AI/AN alone and leave a fuller examination of the results for AI/AN and at least one other race and AI/AN and Hispanic for future research.

9. We group respondents who are Hispanic (and not AI/AN) so that we have mutually exclusive groups.

10. Results are robust to a more inclusive definition of income (available upon request).

11. In this specification, the omitted category includes both high school graduates and those without a high school diploma. The results are robust to including an indicator for high school graduation.

12. This vector includes both exogenous characteristics like age and sex as well as endogenous characteristics that are influenced by the decision to pursue higher education. We do not find that separating these out influences results.

13. Neal and Johnson (1996) argue that estimates of the Black-White earnings gap may be biased by the fact that Black students pursue education at different rates due to their assessment of future labor market discrimination. This logic could extend to AI/AN students and would be an example of a reason to worry about differential selection bias across racial groups. Additionally, we have heard anecdotal evidence that AI/AN women may have different life-cycle patterns with regard to timing of career/school and family/fertility, which could also lead to systematically different human capital accumulation.

14. The universe for the earnings variable is not identical to employment. Results are robust to including all respondents with earnings, even those not currently employed.

15. Results are robust to including part-time workers.

16. Results are robust to including workers with less than $10,000 in earnings (with the exception of when we include both respondents who are not employed and those with less than $10,000 in earnings, in which case we get a different sign on the interaction of Black and BA+.)

17. A related working paper (Keo, Peterson, and West, 2018) by the authors reports separate estimates by geographic characteristics (i.e. urban/rural and whether the PUMA includes a homeland). Geographic location is particularly endogenous to employment (meaning that where you live influences your employment status but your employment status also influences where you live), however, so additional analysis is needed.

18. To be precise, because there are interaction variables, the coefficients on non-White racial groups are the gaps for workers with no postsecondary education and the coefficients on education are the returns for Whites.

19. Appendix Table A4 show the full slate of control variables and disaggregates results of log earnings by gender. We find that the white-AI/AN gap for workers with no college course work (i.e., the main coefficients on AI/AN-alone) is statistically significant only for men. In other words, after controlling for other demographic and geographic differences, female workers with no college who

identify as AI/AN (alone or in combination) have earnings that are, on average, no different from their White peers. In contrast, the earnings gap for workers with no college persists for women from other non-White racial groups.

20. In a robustness check (not shown) we estimate the results separately for each year and find no evidence of favorable (or unfavorable) trends. The disparities are consistent over the time period studied.

21. This difference is statistically significant at the <0.01 level.

22. Appendix Table A5 disaggregates results by gender and shows the full slate of controls. We find that the White-AI/AN employment gap is larger for men than for women, and the marginal return for a BA+ is larger for AI/AN men than AI/AN women. This difference is statistically significant at the <0.01 level.

23. In Appendix Table A6, we disaggregate the LFP results by gender and show full regression results. We find that the LFP gap and the differential returns to a BA+ are larger for men than for women.

24. In a related working paper, we simulate the impact of a hypothetical policy that increases AI/AN college-going and completion rates to match those of Whites to show that policies that increase college going are necessary but not sufficient to close White-AI/AN labor market gaps. In our simulation we estimate that a hypothetical intervention that fully addressed White-AI/AN disparities in higher education would leave White-AI/AN labor market disparities largely unresolved. In other words, interventions that reduce racial gaps in access, persistence, and completion in higher education are necessary but far from sufficient.

REFERENCES

Abel, J., & Dietz, R. (2014). Do the benefits of college still outweigh the costs? *Current Issues in Economics and Finance, 20*(3), 1–9.

Akee, R. K., Copeland, W. E., Keeler, G., Angold, A., & Costello, E. J. (2010). Parents' incomes and children's outcomes: A quasi-experiment using transfer payments from casino profits. *American Economic Journal: Applied Economics, 2*(1), 86–115.

Akee, R., & Yazzie-Mintz, T. (2011). "Counting experience" among the least counted: The role of cultural and community engagement on educational outcomes for American Indian, Alaska Native, and Native Hawaiian students. *American Indian Culture and Research Journal, 35*(3), 119–150.

Angrist, J., & Krueger, A. (1999). Empirical strategies in labor economics. In O. Ashenfelter & D. Card (Eds.), *The handbook of labor economics* (Vol. 3, pp. 1277–1366). New York, NY: Elsevier Science.

Austin, A. (2013). Native Americans and jobs: The challenge and the promise. *EPI Briefing Paper #370*, Economic Policy Institute.

Barrow, L., & Rouse, C. E. (2005). Do returns to schooling differ by race and ethnicity? *American Economic Review, 95*(2), 83–87.

Bertrand, M., and Mullainathan, S. (2004). Are Emily and Greg more employable than Lakisha and Jamal? A field experiment on labor market discrimination. *American Economic Review 94*(4), 991–1013.

Brayboy, B. M. J., Fann, A.J., Castagno, A. E., & Solyom, J.A. (2012). Postsecondary education for American Indian and Alaska Natives: Higher education for nation building and self-determination, *ASHE Higher Education Report* 37(5), 1–154.

Brayboy, B. M. J., Solyom, J. A., & Castagno, A.E. (2015). Indigenous peoples in higher education. *Journal of American Indian Education, 54*(1), 154–186.

Card, D., & Krueger, A. B. (1992). Does school quality matter? Returns to education and the characteristics of public schools in the United States. *Journal of Political Economy 100*(1), 1–40.

Carneiro, P., & Heckman, J. J. (2005). Labor market discrimination and racial differences in premarket factors. *The Journal of Law and Economics 48*(1), 1–39.

Carneiro, P., Heckman, J. J., & Vytlacil, E. J. (2011). Estimating marginal returns to education. *American Economic Review, 101*(6), 2754–81.

Cooper, S., & Cohn, E. (1997). Internal rates of return to college education in the United States by sex and race. *Journal of Education Finance, 23*(1), 101–133.

Corak, M. (2013). Income inequality, equality of opportunity, and intergenerational mobility. *Journal of Economic Perspectives, 27*(3), 79–102.

Cunningham, J. (2007). *The path of many journeys: The benefits of higher education for Native people and communities.* A report by the Institute for Higher Education Policy in collaboration with the American Indian Higher Education Consortium and the American Indian College Fund, February 2007.

Elliot, W., & Nam, I. (2013). Is student debt jeopardizing the short-term financial health of U.S. households? *Federal Reserve Bank of St. Louis Review, 95*(5), 405–24.

Feir, D. L. (2016). The longterm effects of forcible assimilation policy: The case of Indian boarding schools. *Canadian Journal of Economics/Revue canadienne d'economique, 49*(2), 433–480.

Fischer, S., & Stoddard, C. (2013). The academic achievement of American Indians. *Economics of Education Review, 36*, 135–152.

Gaddis, S. M. (2014). Discrimination in the credential society: An audit study of race and college selectivity in the labor market. *Social Forces 93*(3), 1451–1479.

Gitter, R. J., & Reagan, P. B. (2002). Reservation wages: An analysis of the effects of reservations on employment of American Indian men. *The American Economic Review, 92*(4), 1160–1168.

Guillory, R. M., & Wolverton, M. (2008). It's about family: Native American student persistence in higher education. *The Journal of Higher Education, 79*(1), 58–87.

Harmon, C., & Oosterbeek, H. 2003. The returns to education: Microeconomics. *Journal of Economic Surveys, 6*(4), 453–470.

Heckman, J. J. (1998). Detecting discrimination. *Journal of Economic Perspectives 12*(2), 101–116.

Heckman, J. J., Lochner, L. J., & Todd, P. E. (2006). Earnings functions, rates of return and treatment effects: The Mincer equation and beyond. In E. Hanushek & F. Welch (Eds.), *The Handbook of the Economics of Education* (Vol. 1, pp. 307–458). Amsterdam, NL: North-Holland Press.

Hurst, M. (1997). The determinants of earnings differentials for Indigenous Americans: Human capital, location, or discrimination? *The Quarterly Review of Economics and Finance, 37*(4), 787–807.

James, J. (2012). The college wage premium. Federal Reserve Bank of Cleveland. *Economic Commentary,* Number 2012–10, August 8.

Keo C., Peterson, A., & West, K. (2018). Returns to higher education for American Indian and Alaska Native students. *Federal Reserve Bank of Minneapolis-Center for Indian Country Development Working Paper* No. 2018–03.

Kimmel, J. (1997). Rural wages and returns to education: Differences between Whites, Blacks, and American Indians. *Economics of Education Review, 16*(1), 81–96.

Lemieux, T. (2006). Postsecondary education and increasing wage inequality. *American Economic Review, 96*(2), 195–199.

Mayhew, M. J., Rockenbach, A. N., Bowman, N. A., Seifert, T. A., Wolniak, G. C., Pascarella, E. T., & Terenzini, P. T. (2016). Studying college outcomes in the 2000s: Overview and organization of the research (Chapter One). *How college affects students* (Vol. 3, pp. 1–21). San Francisco, CA: Jossey-Bass.

Mincer, J. A. (1974). *Schooling, experience and earnings.* National Bureau of Economic Research.

Monks, J. (2000). The returns to individual and college characteristics: Evidence from the National Longitudinal Survey of Youth. *Economics of Education Review 19*(3), 279–289.

Musu-Gillette, L., de Brey, C., McFarland, J., Hussar, W., Sonnenberg, W., & Wilkinson-Flicker, S. (2017). *Status and trends in the education of racial and ethnic groups 2017.* Washington, DC: U.S. Department of Education.

Neal, D., & Johnson, W. (1996). The role of premarket factors in Black-White wage differences. *Journal of Political Economy, 105*(5), 869–895.

Patrinos, H. A., and Sakellariou, C. N. (1992). North American Indians in the Canadian labour market: A decomposition of wage differentials. *Economics of Education Review, 11*(3), 257–266.

Perna, L. W. (2005). The benefits of higher education: Sex, racial/ethnic and socioeconomic group differences. *The Review of Higher Education, 29*(1), 23–52.

Postsecondary National Policy Institute. (2018). *Native American Students Factsheet.* Accessed: http://pnpi.org/wp-content/uploads/2018/10/Native-American-Students-Factsheet-FINAL_2018.pdf.

Psacharopoulos, G., & Patrinos, H. (2004). Returns to investment in education: A further update. *Education Economics, 12*(2), 111–134

Ruggles, S., Genadek, K., Goeken, R., Grover, J., & Sobek, M. (2015). *Integrated public use microdata series: Version 6.0* [dataset]. Minneapolis, MN: University of Minnesota. http://doi.org/10.18128/D010.V6.0.

Wise, J., Liebler, C., and Todd, R. (2017). Dissimilarity on the career path: The occupational structure of the American Indian/Alaska Native workforce. *Working Paper No. 2017–01.* Center for Indian Country Development.

"There Needs to Be Full Recognition of Who We Are Beyond Symbolic Gestures": Indigenous People's Stories About Their Education and Experiences

ERICA NEEGANAGWEDGIN

This article focuses on 10 Indigenous peoples' reflections on their experiences in Canadian schools. Through government legislation, policies and attitudes, past and present, educational systems have systematically and consistently denied and devalued Indigenous educational systems and ways of being. This article provides insights into the experiences of Indigenous peoples in educational settings where their Indigenous identity was ignored or suppressed. It also recommends ways in which educational systems may be improved to better meet the needs of Indigenous students. The students' stories demonstrate that Indigenous intellectual traditions remain strong, are firmly grounded in the land on which their ancestors lived, and that the honoring of Indigenous lands and territories is at the core of Indigenous well-being and learning.

FOR CENTURIES, INDIGENOUS PEOPLES AND CULTURES within Canada used their own ways of knowing to provide teachings within their respective communities. They were informed by their knowledge systems that are rooted in, and routed through, their ancestral lands and kinship and clan systems. Indigenous knowledges and educational systems are holistic and include the emotional, mental, physical, and spiritual aspects of experience. (Truth and Reconciliation Commission of Canada [TRC], 2015; Royal Commission on Aboriginal People [RCAP], 1996a, 1996b). Yet, the history which Indigenous peoples and settlers have shared has been disruptive and destructive towards Indigenous peoples.

In its 1996 report, the Royal Commission on Aboriginal Peoples (RCAP) called for a new relationship between Indigenous nations and Canada on a nation-to-nation basis. The report said that it was time for all to acknowledge the conflictual history between Indigenous peoples and the Canadian nation-state and to rebuild the relationship on the basis of "honesty, mutual respect, and fair sharing" (p. 1). However, this relationship still remains jagged and imbalanced. The marginalization of Indigenous nations in institutions across Canada, including in the education system, endures. The Kairos Canada (2016, 2017) *Report Card* on Indigenous people's education in Canada shows that, across most Canadian provinces, more work must be done in K–12 schools concerning Indigenous education and, in some provinces (including Ontario), significant work is required in terms of implementation. The Kairos Canada (2018) *Report Card* shows a marked improvement in public commitment and implementation of Indigenous people's perspectives in the curricula, yet much work remains as any commitment and improvement to Canada's Eurocentric curriculum must be ongoing and lifelong. Many Indigenous scholars (Battiste, 2013; Hare, 2011; McGregor, 2013; Metallic, 2008) show that Indigenous education in Canada continues to be integral and important to Indigenous people's lives. The 1972 policy document, "Indian Control of Indian Education," outlines several ways in which Indigenous peoples would like to implement their own educational systems (National Indian Brotherhood/Assembly of First Nations, 1972). The assertion of Indigenous treaty rights and governance concerning Indigenous education continues today.

The purpose of this research is to examine the educational experiences of 10 self-identified Indigenous students, all of whom were attending postsecondary institutions in Canada at the time of this research. In this article, "schooling" refers to any formal environment in which the participants attended and formal learning occurred. By examining the experiences of the students, the article is intended to reveal some of the challenges the public-school system presents for Indigenous students, and possibilities for improvement. This research and analysis may be used to bring about positive, fundamental and practical policy changes.

Understanding of Self as Researcher

As a Taino/racialized person who lives on Indigenous lands in Canada and works within the education system, I have tried to center the experiences of Indigenous peoples in the Canadian context through shared stories. I have a multifaceted understanding of Indigeneity and Indigenous knowledge systems from the local and global contexts, and an understanding of the impact of colonialism. Battiste (2013) notes that

"Indigenous people in Canada, and Indigenous peoples throughout the world, are feeling the tensions which were created by a Eurocentric education system that has taught them to distrust their Indigenous knowledge systems" (p. 24). Shreve (2015) adds that the development of a global Indigenous consciousness stems from Indigenous peoples' common colonial experience. The author explains that "in the 15th century, European powers sliced and parcelled up nearly every corner of the globe, resulting in unprecedented dispossession, death, and destruction for Indigenous peoples" (para. 4). I am familiar with this impact, given the history of genocide of Indigenous peoples which began on our ancestral Caribbean lands in 1492. This history demonstrates the attempt to annihilate Caribbean peoples from our ancestral territories, yet we live and carry on.

I am committed to Indigenous education for many reasons. First, it is important for me, as someone who lives and works on Indigenous lands, to recognize the inherent and treaty rights of Indigenous peoples, and to know and remember whose ancestral lands and territories I am on. This is part of my commitment to not willingly participate in the oppression of Indigenous peoples as I develop my understanding of the ways in which people beyond those from the dominant culture see their world. My commitment to Indigenous education stems from seeing the continuing consequences of this history in Indigenous peoples' lives. Bishop (2005) explains this as (identifying) "through culturally appropriate means, your bodily linkage, your engagement, and, therefore, an unspoken but implicit commitment to other people" (p. 118). I view this as part of the process of developing a critical awareness which sometimes involves tension. Those who propose "other" ways of knowing are often met with displays of violence. For example, as a person who has both Indigenous Taino and African ancestry, I have found that the Taino peoples have been depicted as no longer existing.

As someone who works within a postsecondary context, I have found that many individuals often don't know about Indigenous peoples but are familiar with the names of European explorers and colonialists (Bigelow, 1998). This is structural violence in the education system, and the story in the schools remains the same regardless of the geographical location. The cycle of systemic challenges continues and is often generational as younger children hear these selective histories. The research in this article privileges Indigenous voices and their understanding of their experiences.

Research Methods

This research uses Indigenous pedagogy of story-telling and knowledge-sharing. Cajete (2015) explains the significance of Indigenous stories and remembering, stating that "to remember is also a way to re-know and reclaim a part of our lives" (p. 2). Pete, Schneider, and O'Reilly (2013) assert that stories are sources of knowledge and are acts of resistance, while Corntassel (2012) states that "Remembering is resistance" (p. 86). This is significant given that Canadian government policies were meant to erase Indigenous people's culture, knowledge and identity. Cajete (2015) writes about the danger of outside sources and interference, but asserts that dialogue counters those forces and helps to stimulate the research which we participate in. He describes this form of research as "rooted" since it is remembering history, revives our memories and creates new stories.

The research for this article was carried out between 2009 and 2012. During that time, six of the participants completed high school and started attending universities, while four had been out of high school for five years or more. The ten participants in this study identify from various Indigenous nations including Métis, Anishinabek, and Cree nations within Canada; they reflected on their experiences in high school and postsecondary settings. They had attended schools in several Canadian provinces including Ontario, British Columbia, Saskatchewan, Alberta, Newfoundland, and Labrador. The participants were interviewed individually; some chose to be interviewed in person while others preferred telephone interviews. Each interview ranged from 45 to 90 minutes, and each participant provided permission for the interview to be recorded. Research Ethics Board protocol review and approval were provided for this work. Pseudonyms are used throughout the text to protect the participants' identities and ensure their anonymity.

This study was guided by two central research questions (framed as questions for participants):

1. Can you describe your schooling and classroom experiences in any formal school context?
2. What do you think that Indigenous education should look like?

These research questions helped to capture the essence of each participant's experiences and stories. Interviewing participants, engaging and sharing in dialogue and conversation is an Indigenous approach which aligns with Indigenous worldviews (Kovach, 2009). The interview data were organized into themes derived from the responses regarding schooling.

Discussion and Themes

The following four themes emerged from this research. The first is the importance of land and the relationship that Indigenous people have with their land. The second theme relates to the history of schooling for Indigenous youth and its impact. The third is the *othering* and singling out of Indigenous children in schools today. The fourth theme is the importance of centering Indigenous ways of knowing. These themes overlap and intersect with each other.

Theme 1: Importance of and Relationship to Land

Two students, Jenny and Kelly, addressed this topic. Jenny commented,

> I remember singing these horrible songs about Native people. I am like, why do I know these songs by heart? One song, I think it was from Peter Pan . . . sweet and good I did what I could, and I called my shack, break my back but the land was sweet and good.

The use of this song marginalizes Indigenous students within schools. It presents the question of whose land was sweet and good, especially given Canada's history of methodically displacing Indigenous peoples from their lands.

This illustrates the way in which Eurocentric worldviews dominate school settings, and it speaks to Canada's ongoing systemic violence towards Indigenous peoples, starting with their lands. Singing these songs to children normalizes the theft of Indigenous lands. Non-Indigenous people must recognize that they are on Indigenous lands. Acknowledging Indigenous lands have been part of Indigenous peoples' protocol and code of ethics since time immemorial. Currently, there is a movement toward that realization as many schools across Canada engage in recognizing the land on which their school is located. Indigenous peoples often initiate and lead these crucial efforts.

Battiste (2013) calls on us to "imagine the consequences of a powerful ideology that positions one group as superior and gives away First Nations peoples' lands and resources and invite churches and other administrative agents to occupy their homeland, while negating their very existence and finally moving them from the Canadian landscape to lands no one wants" (p. 23). These points are significant but are often absent from educational institutions across Canada. Many schools are implicated in the disregarding and suppression of Indigenous peoples by their omission of Indigenous peoples. The contemporary education system remains a source of trauma for many Indigenous peoples by perpetuating mistruths and omissions about Indigenous peoples.

Metallic (2008) says of the Mi'kmaq people that "we've always lived from our lands" (p. 60). This is because many aspects of Indigenous peoples' rights and intellectual systems are inherent to their lands and knowledge systems, have always existed and were given to them by the Creator.

Another participant, Kelly, noted,

> There can be no true reconciliation without having our land back. Land claims take years to settle with the government and, in the end, we continue to lose our land. Ceded or unceded, we never gave up our land. Our treaty rights are often ignored yet we are Indigenous peoples. There needs to be full recognition of who we are beyond symbolic gestures. Treaties were signed nation to nation, and they continue to undermine that fact. Our land is precious to us, our sacred sites are undeniably part of who we are, and this will never change.

These comments highlight Indigenous people's connection and relationship with their territories and reinforce the impact of the colonial history.

The RCAP (1996b), discussing the close relationships and meaning of the land to Indigenous peoples, stated that, "Aboriginal people have told us of their special relationship to the land and its resources. This relationship, they say, is both spiritual and material, not only one of livelihood, but of community and indeed of the continuity of their cultures and societies" (p. 438). This shows the strong connection that Indigenous people traditionally had with their lands and the meaning of the land for them. To contextualize the impact of land displacement, Indigenous reserve land base constitutes only 0.2% of all lands in Canada. (Department of Indigenous and Northern Affairs Canada, 2018).

It must also be understood that Indigenous peoples have an intimate and reciprocal relationship with their lands (RCAP, 1996b). Therefore, the land is seen as a relative and is not to be possessed and violated. Further, Cajete (2015) explains that "When Native peoples interact with the place where we have lived for generations, the landscape becomes a reflection of our very soul" (p. 48). In fact, Indigenous care of the land and their relationship with their lands are imbedded in their legal traditions and ways of life and are passed down from the ancestors (Rose, 1996). I can relate to Indigenous people from Turtle Island who talk about their connection with their ancestral lands. I know what it is like to feel a deep connection to the land which can be felt within your heart. In fact, we have a kinship relationship with the land. McGregor, Bayha, and Simmonds (2010) remind us of how the experience of being on the land with family, and learning about one's responsibilities, is central to Indigenous worldviews. Jenny reinforces this opinion of public school, stating,

> You know, I would like it to be a place where we can challenge people. That is what I think would be helpful. I think it is challenging but that is what I would need—I guess what I would need is, straight off the bat, this is Native land you know. This is Native land. It has to be really connected to land. Sovereignty has to be connected to land.

Having a land base is part of Indigenous people's right to self-determination. This is supported by The United Nations *Declaration on the Rights of Indigenous Peoples* (UNDRIP), which speaks to the concern of the General Assembly that

> indigenous peoples have suffered from historic injustices as a result of, inter alia, their colonization and dispossession of their lands, territories and resources, thus preventing them from exercising, in particular, their right to development in accordance with their own needs and interests. (United Nations General Assembly, 2007, p. 3)

Cajete (2015) notes that "to understand Indigenous Education, we must consider not only community and culture but also land, which is the first and most essential teacher and community member and the origin of Indigenous cultures" (p. 46). Similarly, Spillett reminds us that Indigenous land-based education is premised on the understanding that knowledge comes through the land and "we are inherently connected to our territories that land can be a text and land can be a teacher from an informing knowledge transmission" (CBC Indigenous Live, 2016). The connection between land and Indigenous intellectual traditions is such that Indigenous people's holistic relationship to their lands is essential and cannot be minimized.

Theme 2: The History of Schooling for Indigenous Peoples

Residential schools figure prominently in the harm which was done to Indigenous children. During Canada's use of residential schools, which was forced on Indigenous peoples, many Indigenous children were torn from their ancestral lands. Participants Ava, Kris and Jan spoke about the ways in which Canada's residential schools affected them, their families and their communities.

Ava commented that she went on a tour with her sister. She continued to say that

> after the tour . . . my sister and I were standing outside, and she pointed at the building and she said "that's the Residential School." She said, "Do you know what they say? They say that you can still hear the children crying down in the basement." My mother was there, and my brother was there, and my sister was there, but I guess the rest of us went to school in the city. I guess because of Children's Aid.

When asked if she was ever able to go back to her mother after being taken by Children Services, Ava stated, "I went back, I guess when she won me back. You know, like she had to go to court for me."

Ava's comments refer to pain, hardship and the horrors of residential schools; thus, a discussion of the schools' history, although well documented, is necessary. Under the Canadian nation-state, Indigenous education, including residential schools, served as a systemic effort to erase Indigenous forms of cultural transmission. Christian missionaries were the first outsiders to impose their formal education system upon Indigenous peoples. This was done with the intention of "civilizing" the children so that they conformed to Christianity and settlers' ways. (Hare, 2011, p. 95). The first missionary-operated schools in New France (now Canada) were established in the 1620s (Frideres, 2011). Haig-Brown (2012) noted that "sporadic and geographically focused efforts to use schools to influence Indigenous children were developed from the 1600s, but it was not until the mid-1800s that British North America undertook a systemic investigation into the use of residential schools to serve the goals of assimilation" (p. 223).

Ava's story, above, described a cycle of systemic oppression which the colonial system created. Children were forced into residential schools and later, in the 1960s, generations of children were taken by Children's Aid Services (CAS). Ava's mother then fought to get her daughter back through the court system which had historically and still has today a history of demonizing Indigenous peoples. The history of CAS across Canada, removing Indigenous children from their families during the 1960s, became known as the 60s scoop. This system persists today and is known as the millenial scoop.

The ideologies that influenced the removal of Indigenous children in Canada historically are still at play today in their removal from their homes into Canada's child welfare system. This is not by accident, however; it is systemic and part of the assimilation process to "get them while they are young." This is because adults were not just considered irredeemable but were a hindrance to the assimilation process (Milloy, 1999). The effects of Canada's assimilationist and violent policies have been vast for Indigenous peoples, and they continue to harm Indigenous families and communities. Milloy (1999) writes that residential school connects to other institutions including child welfare, health care and prisons. The 1960s scoop, for example, resulted from Canadian policies which were said to be in the "best interest of the child" (Milloy, 1999, p. xxi).

During the residential school years, parents were shattered by the separation from their children. One participant, Kris, who had spent years in a residential school, said that the children did not understand what was happening when Canadian government officials came to take siblings away from his family. Their mother did not say a word but sobbed uncontrollably. Kris later asked why she had sent them to the school. His mother replied that she had no choice. However, it was not until his mother's death that Kris fully came to understand that his parents had little choice about the children attending the residential school.

Kris explained that his parents were in shock when the children were sent away. He stated, "When we got on the plane, my mother threw herself on the grass and lay there crying. I was told she cried there for hours." After arriving in the city, the siblings were separated. Kris said, "I hung onto my sibling's leg and did not want to let go." First-hand accounts of experiences within these schools demonstrate the bewilderment of the children who wondered why their parents sent them to these schools.

Bennett, Blackstock, and De La Ronde (2005) add that being removed from their homes and forced to live in strange and abusive settings was traumatic for the children. However, this removal of Indigenous children from their homes was part of the government's plan. The ongoing effects of this system had major consequences not only for the children and their parents, but also for their extended families, communities, systems of education, governance and overall way of life.

Once in these schools, the children were further marginalized by many of those who ran the schools. Acts of physical, sexual and psychological violence were notorious features of residential schools and have been well-documented. (TRC, 2012, 2015). Kris described repeatedly witnessing abuse of a child by the nuns and priests who were in charge of the school. He noted that, "We used to take him under our wings. We tried to protect ourselves to keep them away from us and we tried to protect him." Children resisted by doing what they could to protect each other.

In the Truth and Reconciliation Commission (TRC) of Canada (2012) *Interim Report,* Commissioners Justice Murray Sinclair (chair), Chief Wilton Littlechild, and Marie Wilson provide startling statistics of the detrimental history of residential schools, including the reality that at least one in 25 Indigenous children were killed in these schools. In comparison, one in 26 Canadian soldiers died in World War II (TRC, 2012).

Jan, another participant, stated, "My mother was one of the people that was in residential school where she was abused there and, when she came out of residential school, I believe she didn't know how to mother any of us." This shows the intensity of the government's policies which led to the destruction of families. In many cases, parents never had the chance to see their children again. The purpose of the system of residential schools—"to kill the Indian in the child"—was obvious. Government policies were systemic, and the deaths in schools were essentially genocide. In fact, the government stopped recording deaths because the numbers were so high (Miller, 2017). This was done to avoid future implications, such as families seeking justice.

The Truth and Reconciliation Council (2015) corroborates this, stating that "tens of thousands of Aboriginal children for over a century . . . were torn from their parents, who often surrendered them only under threat of prosecution. And they were hurled into a strange and frightening place, one in which their parents and culture would be demeaned and oppressed" (p. 37). Residential schools became the schooling model for Indigenous children and youth across Canada, with the law requiring that parents send their children to these schools. Ava's story is remarkable, though, for her mother challenging the system (i.e., the CAS and Canadian courts). Despite having attended residential school, Ava's mother fought to get her daughter back. The participants recount a history of Indigenous resistance to government policies.

Dickason and McNab (2009) explain that, from the start of the residential school system, Indigenous peoples "fought and sought to counteract what they rightly recognized as trauma and an attempt at cultural assimilation" (p. 308). They also comment that parents protested, and children resisted by running away from these schools. Kris noted that he ran away numerous times and school officials became frustrated and angry. Dickason and McNab note that "families pitched their tents just beyond the grounds of school in order to be close to their children and facilitate visiting them" (pp. 308–309).

Many participants expressed how being able to talk about their experience helped them to start their journey of healing. These residential schools were intended to bring about the end of Indigenous people as a distinct group within Canadian society and that effort failed (Truth and Reconciliation Commission of Canada, 2012).

Theme 3: Contemporary Education Experiences: "Being Singled Out"

The history and experiences of residential school described are also connected to the institutionalized discrimination which Indigenous students experience in contemporary schooling (Battiste, 2013; RCAP, 1996b; TRC, 2015). Participants Stace and Julie discussed the challenges of being singled out in school. Stace commented,

> The worst thing about school was the fact that when, especially in history class—I'm talking elementary and middle school—whenever we would do history and we would talk about Native people and people would be like wow, did Native people really do that? Everyone always singles me out, always.

Julie added,

> You know what because I remember we were in our law class and they were talking about Native people and whenever they talked about Native people, there was me and a couple of Native kids—they're from way up North. The things they would say. . . . Even one of the teachers singled us Native people out.

Toulouse (2014) outlines several approaches to the ways in which Indigenous peoples teach their children, emphasizing the importance of both Elders and extended families to Indigenous learning and teaching.

Toulouse explains, "Experiential learning, oral tradition, and land-based experiences ensured the continuity and survival of Aboriginal groups, their knowledge, and culture. Children's learning was fluid, and learning opportunities were part of a seamless process from birth through to adulthood" (p. 21). Cajete (2015) discusses the importance of stories, explaining that "story is how we frame information and experience within a context that makes them meaningful" (p. 95), while Williams (2011) states that "the land remembers and constructs relationships with those who live on it" (p. vi). Therefore, traditionally, Indigenous children would be educated in an environment with which they were familiar, with family and friends with whom they were familiar. There would have been no "singling out."

Cajete (2015) notes that "in very different ways, contemporary schooling has targeted Indigenous knowledges for demise." (p. 170). According to Madden, Higgins, and Korteweg (2013), even a brief introduction to the education of Indigenous students in Canada reveals a web of systemic injustice that schools maintain through educational hegemony (p. 218). Indigenous children are often disregarded. These shared discussions of being singled out in the classroom has emerged as a tenet of contemporary schooling in many classrooms across Canada and supports previous studies (Snively & Williams, 2016).

In non-Indigenous schools, Indigenous students experience various forms of unaccustomed spotlighting, from being different from the majority, to being singled out for learning activities, to punishment and praise. Persistent marginalization inevitably follows (Sharifian, 2011). Another participant, Julie, shared similar experiences noting the following:

> I remember being in grade nine and my history teacher singling me out and I forget what it was, but it was something along the lines of, something about Native people, and I remember the teacher saying, I know who's going to have an opinion on this, and then he put me on the spot. Me being so shy and so you know, not knowing about Native people, I felt so stupid you know what I mean. Like I don't know any of the history, this is the first time that I have ever been exposed to anything like really in a textbook that you know, where they ask me my opinion you know.

Singling out Indigenous students in the classroom ignores the fact that Indigenous peoples are diverse with many different cultures and languages. In Canada there are over 600 First Nations on reserve communities. Not everyone will know their history, yet students are expected to be experts and teach the teacher. According to Hamill (2015), singling out students individually can be intimidating, whereas an open discussion can lead to co-operative and collective understanding.

There is a lack of historical knowledge in Canada, but also a denial of the history of colonialism and of the genocidal policies and actions against Indigenous peoples under Canada's policies. These policies and actions were intended to erase Indigenous governance systems and impose Canada's own systems. This cuts across all Canadian institutions, including education. This denial and forgetfulness extend to Canada's systemic historical and ongoing attempt to erase Indigenous peoples' culture and history. The TRC (2015) refers to this as cultural genocide.

These experiences demonstrate the need to ensure that Indigenous perspectives are implemented in a meaningful way in all schools and classrooms. Many of the participants speak to the need to challenge Eurocentric tyranny and to center Indigenous ways of knowing as a way to move education into the future.

Theme 4: The Importance of Centering Indigenous Ways of Knowing

Centering Indigenous ways of knowing is critical as education boards and schools throughout Canada respond to the TRC (2015) calls to action on education in Canada. Mace shares her perspective of what Indigenous peoples' centering their ways of knowing within the school curriculum looks and feels like in the following comments:

> What I liked most about the curriculum is that we did a lot of circle sharing that gave each student a chance to speak and to be heard. I find that technique was very good because it created a bond with the student. We were all brothers and sisters, you all understood exactly how you felt and then knowing how that person feels, then you know what to talk about. You know you're not going to talk about something that hurts someone. You're not going to talk about things that are going to upset others because by sharing in the circle you're getting to know each person personally. You're learning from them also, and another thing is the age bracket. They had from young to old. You are learning from the young while the young are learning from the old.

Each participant in the research for this study shared their view that Indigenous systems such as sharing circle help to create a bond and a collaborative learning space which is built on reciprocity and relationship building. These systems are linked to Indigenous views of the world. Lambe (2003) notes that people do not argue about what is correct or who has the truth. It is up to the person, and his or her own interpretations, to decide what is appropriate. This reflects the ethics and worldviews within Indigenous education.

Jenny said of the curriculum within Canadian schools:

> I want a shakedown. I would like to see First Nations curriculum. I mean I still think you can meet the Provincial standards right, but I think it can be done from an Anishinaabe worldview . . . and that's starting to happen. History needs to be written from a First Nations point of view in this country.

This is a call to remember Anishinabek ways of knowing. Cherubini (2014) discusses the prominence of Eurocentrism in schools, adding that "despite various attempts on changing these experiences for Indigenous students, public school classrooms often continue to promote Eurocentric educational principles, which fail to recognize the legitimacy of Aboriginal epistemologies or to adequately incorporate them into curricula" (p. 3). Hare (2011) maintains that the education of Indigenous peoples must be understood within the colonial framework that was intent on eliminating the "Indian problem" and in the context of the inequalities which are inherent in the educational system (p. 91). Those inequalities challenge the educational success of Indigenous children and youth. Jenny's wanting a "shakedown" reinforces the need to understand the systemic and epistemic violence in curricula and the necessity for change.

Melissa, another participant, noted,

> I don't know why they don't put more Cree content in the curriculum. Our teacher, when we were going to school, was also from another nearby community and there was a lot of stuff that he found in the history books that were very degrading. . . . He would say, "I don't want anyone to say this word in the classroom. Because of its impact." He says there are some words you have to ignore in this history book.

According to Toulouse (2014), First Nations, Métis and Inuit students' self-esteem is grounded in classrooms where they recognize themselves in the curriculum with its resources, teachings, strategies, histories and knowledge exchanges. This supports one participant's experience when the school environment honored and respected Indigenous ways of doing. The participant emphasizes the need to put First Nations languages first. Many Indigenous peoples are working to revitalize their languages which are important to their identities. Julie says of the school curriculum:

> They never understood or mention in the history about the ecosystems, the damage they did or are doing. It never occurs to them that we always practiced in good ways. It's not written anywhere in the history books that we never tried to kill everything at once just to make money. We made sure, there was something there when we went back the following year. They don't teach that stuff in the history books.

Menjivar (2017) says of schooling and educational settings that "They are institutions and practices that exist and operate on stolen land and have been founded through violence, genocide and white supremacy. They are cut from the same cloth, and thus are designed to inform, mirror and reflect those same principles, processes, practices, tools and tactics" (para. 12). Battiste (2013) warns that, "Decolonizing Indigenous education first and foremost must be framed within concepts of dialogue, respect for educational pluralities, multiplicities, and diversities. It is about self-determination, deconstructing the decisions about curricular knowledge, and re-energizing education and knowledge to the contexts of lives" (p. 107).

According to Harrington and CHiXapkaid (Pavel) (2013), mainstream educational systems impede Indigenous students' academic achievement. Battiste (2013) adds that, "Public schools are not politically neutral sites" (p. 96), and that those holding political power control knowledge and have the power to exclude knowledge from curricula. For this reason, Jenny wishes to challenge the current system and assert Indigenous rights. As she says,

> I would really like to have Native experiences centered. I would really like to have the issues put on the table and confronted. I would really like attention drawn to dynamics in the classroom. You know, like questions posed like why is it that people who are not Native feel so confident talking about experiences that aren't their own.

Challenging people who speak about Indigenous experiences, and who co-opt it, undermines it and reflects power relations. It is a call for people to reflect on and challenge their own perceptions and conjectures of Indigenous people in schools. This is why Indigenous people have shown concern for their children's education and understand their connection to education.

McCarty, Borgoiakova, Gilmore, Lomawaima, and Romero-Little (2005) reinforce the fact that Indigenous peoples throughout North America work to determine their children's education. They note that they

> also believe that Native individuals, communities, schools, and nations are sincerely working to imagine new kinds of education based on Indigenous systems of knowledge and practice. Though burdened by centuries of repression, marginalization, and negation, they are working to reinvoke and reinvent educational systems based on centuries-old wellsprings of experience and intellectual engagement. (p. 4)

Implications of the Findings

Indigenous people across Canada are breaking down institutional barriers and colonial structures to ensure that their education systems are not discounted. Indigenous peoples, parents and communities throughout Canada have established schools because they are aware of the trauma that schools can cause for their children. (As one example, the former First Nations Junior and Senior School of Toronto now under its newly reclaimed name Kapapamahchakwew - Wandering Spirit School. "teaches the Ontario Curriculum while centering Indigenous knowledge, perspectives and cultures"; see https://schoolweb.tdsb.on.ca/FNST). Tessa, another participant, notes that "efforts by our communities to educate our children using our own learning systems continue. This is despite the disruption and policies by the government to prevent cultural transmission and undermining of our people and their knowledges." Julie suggested,

> They should put more Native content in the classrooms and at the same time there was a school in one of the northern communities where they take out one week and learn traditional ways. They take students out and they go hunt geese, they learn those things. This is what I mean that maybe you have Elders go in there. Just because a teacher went to university doesn't mean they know.

Indigenous pedagogy serves as a reminder of Indigenous forms of governance and self-determination in education. It is also a reminder that, in some schools, Indigenous cultures, languages and intellectual traditions have continued and are structured and centered alongside the provincial curriculum. They are not just included as nominal requirements.

Discussion and Policy: Looking Ahead

This study adds new Indigenous voices to the discussion of education, and it should inform practical and policy changes. The topics that emerged emphasize the ideas that attention must be paid to Indigenous systems of education, to the relationship between Indigenous people and their lands, to the history and impact of education in Canada, to the effects of singling out Indigenous peoples, and to Indigenous self-determination through Indigenous education. Indigenous voices must be prioritized in policy. Through both the *Indian Control of Indian Education* policy document of 1972 and the voices of the participants in this study, Indigenous peoples have been calling for changes. They continue to do so in their communities. For example, the report of the Truth and Reconciliation Commission of Canada (2015) includes 94 calls to action, including calls for "federal, provincial and territorial governments, in consultation and collaboration with survivors, Aboriginal peoples, and educators to make age-appropriate curricula on residential schools, Treaties, and Aboriginal peoples' historical and contemporary contributions to Canada a mandatory education requirement for Kindergarten to Grade Twelve students" (p. 7).

The Ontario Ministry of Education (2018), in response to the TRC calls-to-action No. 62 and No. 63 on Education, and in collaboration with Indigenous peoples and communities, recently started the process of revising their curriculum to include Indigenous history, residential school and the legacy of colonialism. The Province of Alberta also revised its curriculum to honour the TRC's calls to action, noting that "current and future Kindergarten to Grade 12 curricula in Alberta must include student learning outcomes specific to First Nations, Métis and Inuit perspectives and experiences, as well as content on the significance of residential schools and treaties" (Alberta Education, 2018, p. 1).

Since the summer of 2018, the new government in Ontario has cancelled the upcoming revisions to the K–12 curricula on including Indigenous scholarship within the curricula. The fact that revisions have been cancelled (see Maracle, 2018) speaks to the need for ongoing commitment, and it emphasizes the paternalistic nature of contemporary colonial governments that continue to exert control on Indigenous communities.

The findings in this research call for centering Indigenous ways of knowing and being, and for the prioritization and normalization of Indigenous-focused curricula in all subject areas and across all grades K–12 within these systems. The Ontario Ministry of Education and other ministries across Canada have a responsibility to ensure not only that social studies has Indigenous-focused content, but mathematics, science and other subject areas must also be included. To honor the voices and stories of Indigenous peoples, the ministries of education across the country need to privilege the stories and experiences of Indigenous peoples throughout its curricula. The revision of the curriculum needs to be alive, continuous and ongoing, and teachers have a responsibility to do so both individually and collectively. The curriculum ought to significantly reflect the history and contemporary experiences of Indigenous peoples. It must include yesterday, today and tomorrow and should be done in respectful ways. Education policies should recognize Indigenous voices and inform practices. According to Jacob (2018), policy is always situated in a web of social power. This means policy makers should recognize the power relations that exist in their policy-making roles. Therefore, curriculum changes must result in institutionalized transformation.

Battiste (2013) states that we all have knowledge. However, "the group that controls the meanings and diffusion of knowledge exercises power and privilege over other groups" (p. 96). Those with control then link the diffusion of knowledge with economics, ensuring that some kinds of knowledge are linked to rewards and other kinds of knowledge are not. This speaks to the question of why more Cree content is not in the curriculum. This question is a call-to-action by a Cree student, and policy makers must listen.

Hare (2011) notes, "The responsibility rests with all of us to create space for Indigenous knowledge in learning settings; we must all open our minds as well as our hearts to the different ways knowledge is constructed, shared and valued if education is to benefit all students" (p. 104). Therefore, those who work within a Eurocentric dominant framework must listen to what Indigenous peoples say about their education. Everyone is responsible for dismantling the dominant structures that remain in place, and individuals have a responsibility to avoid reproducing these structures. This requires self-reflection and interrogation of the systems and ways in which dominance is produced, maintained, and normalized.

Conclusion

Previous recommendations of the RCAP (1996a, 1996b) on curricula that reflect Indigenous cultures and community have been taken up across Canada at local levels. This is most apparent where public, independent, and First Nations schools worked with First Nations, Métis, and Inuit family and community members to develop curricula, programs, and services that are based on local Indigenous knowledge (Archibald & Hare, 2016, p. 10). This demonstrates the fact that it is Indigenous people themselves who can best determine how their education systems must look. Implementing this should not be problematic. Indigenous peoples are self-governing peoples and they know what is best for their children.

The TRC (2015) calls to action to redress the legacy of residential schools emphasize the need for commitment. Canada's Residential schools were established to undermine and destroy Indigenous peoples' inherent and treaty rights and their humanity. In referencing these calls for action, I also reflect on Battiste's (2013, p. 77) comments that reconciliation is rooted first in the principle that First Nations parents have a right to have educational choice for their children. That includes the foundations of their own knowledge systems, which enable them to benefit from the lessons in their daily lives.

Erica Neeganagwedgin *is assistant professor at Western University. Her areas of research and teaching include Indigenous epistemologies, Indigenous research methods, Indigenous history and educational policies, history of Indigenous education in North American contexts, and identity and comparative historical race/cultural relations in North America. She enjoys working collaboratively with communities.*

REFERENCES

Alberta Education (2018). First Nations, Metis and Inuit education/Education for reconciliation. Retrieved January 27, 2019 from https://education.alberta.ca/first-nations-m%C3%A9tis-and-Inuit-education/education-for-reconciliation/?searchMode=3.

Archibald, J. Q'um Q'um Xiiem, & Hare, J. (2016, October 24). Indigenizing education in Canada: University of British Columbia: Background Paper for RCAP. Retrieved January 27, 2019 from http://www.queensu.ca/sps/sites/webpublish.queensu.ca.spswww/files/files/Events/Conferences/RCAP/Papers/Archibald_Hare_Indigenizing_Education.pdf.

Battiste, M. (2013). *Decolonizing education: Nourishing the learning spirit*. Saskatoon, SK: Purich.

Bennett, M., Blackstock, C. & De La Ronde, R. (2005). *A literature review and annotated bibliography on aspects of Aboriginal child welfare in Canada* (2nnd ed.). Ottawa, ON: First Nations Child and Family Caring Society of Canada Inc. Retrieved January 27, 2019 from http://cwrp.ca/sites/default/files/publications /en/AboriginalCWLitReview_2ndEd.pdf.

Bigelow, B. (1998). Discovering Columbus: Rereading the past. In B. Bigelow & B. Peterson (Eds.), *Rethinking Columbus: The next 500 years* (pp. 10–11). Milwaukee, WI: Rethinking Schools.

Bishop, R. (2005). Freeing ourselves from neo-colonial domination in research. A Kaupapa Māori approach to creating knowledge. In N. K. Denzin & Y. S. Lincoln (Eds.), *The SAGE handbook of qualitative research* (3rd ed.) (pp. 109–138). Thousand Oaks, CA: SAGE.

Cajete, G. (2015). *Indigenous community: Rekindling the teaching s of the seventh fire*. St. Paul, MN: Living Justice Press.

CBC Indigenous Live (Leonard Monkman, producer). (2016, June 23). Winnipeg, land based education: Tasha Spillett and Kevin Lamoureux. Retrieved from https://www.facebook.com/CBC.caIndigenous/vieos/indigenous-educators -kevin-lamoureux-and-tasha-spillet-have-some-big-ideas-n-ho/1291742914 186465/

Cherubini, L. (2014). *Aboriginal student engagement and achievement: Educational practices and cultural sustainability*. Vancouver, BC: UBC Press.

Corntassel, J. (2012). Living in a longer now: Moving beyond the state-centric system. In Waziyatawin & M. Y. Bird (Eds.), *For Indigenous minds only: A decolonization handbook* (2nd ed.) (pp. 85–98). Santa Fe, NM: School for Advanced Research Press.

Department of Indigenous and Northern Affairs Canada (2018). Retrieved January 27, 2019 from https://www.aadnc-aandc.gc.ca/eng/1100100034846 /1100100034847.

Dickason, O., & McNab, D. (2009). Leading to an administrative shift. In O. Dickason & D. McNab (Eds.), *Canada's First Nations; A history of founding peoples from earliest times* (4th ed., pp. 288–335). Oxford, UK: Oxford University Press.

Frideres, J. (2011). *First Nations in the twenty-first century*. Oxford, UK: Oxford University Press.

Haig-Brown, C. (2012) Always remembering: Indian residential schools in Canada, In K. Burnett. & G. Read, *Aboriginal history: A reader* (pp. 221–232). Oxford, UK: Oxford University Press.

Hamill, C. (2015). Music. In J. Reyhner (Ed.), *Teaching Indigenous students: Honoring place, community, and culture* (pp. 123–131). Norman, OK: University of Oklahoma Press.

Hare, J. (2011). Learning from Indigenous knowledge in education. In D. Long & O. Dickason, *Visions of the heart: Canadian Aboriginal issues* (3rd ed., pp. 90–108). Oxford, UK: Oxford University Press.

Harrington, B.G. & CHiXapkaid (D. M. Pavel) (2013). Using Indigenous educational research to transform mainstream Education: A guide for P–12 school leaders, *American Journal of Education, 119*(4), 487–511.

Jacob, M. (2018). Indigenous studies speaks to American sociology: The need for individual and social transformations of Indigenous education in the USA. *Social Sciences, 7*(1), 1.

Kairos Canada. (2016, October). Report card: Provincial and territorial curriculum on Indigenous peoples. Retrieved January 30, 2019 from http://www.kairos canada.org/product/education-report-card.

Kairos Canada. (2017, January). Report card: Provincial and territorial curriculum on Indigenous peoples. Retrieved January 27, 2019 from https://www.kairos canada.org/wp-content/uploads/woocommerce_uploads/2015/12/Education -for-Reconciliation-Report-January-2017-FINAL.pdf.

Kairos Canada. (2018, October 9). *Revised report card: Provincial and territorial curriculum on Indigenous peoples.* Retrieved January 27, 2019 from https://www .kairoscanada.org/what-we-do/indigenous-rights/windsofchange-report -cards.

Kovach, M. (2009). *Indigenous methodologies: Characteristics, conversations and contexts.* Toronto, ON: University of Toronto Press.

Lambe, J. (2003). Indigenous education, mainstream education, and Native studies: Some considerations when incorporating Indigenous pedagogy into Native studies. *American Indian Quarterly, 27*(1/2), 308–324.

Madden, B., Higgins, M., & Korteweg, L. (2013). Role models can't just be on posters: Re/membering Bbarriers to Indigenous community engagement. *Canadian Journal of Education, 36*(2), 212–247.

Maracle, D. (2018). Ontario mustn't backslide on education about Indigenous issues. *Ottawa Citizen,* October 25. Retrieved January 27, 2019 from https:// ottawacitizen.com/opinion/columnists/maracle-ontario-mustnt-backslide -on-education-about-indigenous-issues.

McCarty, T. L. Borgoiakova, T., Gilmore, P., Lomawaima, K. T., and Romero, M. E. (2005). Indigenous Epistemologies and education: Self-determination, anthropology, and human rights. *Anthropology and Education Quarterly, 36*(1), 1–7.

McGregor, D. (2013). Toward a paradigm of Indigenous collaboration for geographic research in Canadian environmental and resource management. In J. Johnson & S. Larsen (Eds.), *A deeper sense of place: Stories and journeys of collaboration in Indigenous research* (pp. 157–178). Corvallis, OR: Oregon State University Press.

McGregor, D., Bayha, W., & Simmonds, D. (2010). "Our responsibility to keep the land alive": Voices of Northern Indigenous researchers. *Pimatisiwin: A Journal of Aboriginal and Indigenous Community Health, 8*(1), 101–123.

Menjivar, J.A. (2017). A break-up letter with academia: Not your token guinea pig, show pony, or likable person. Retrieved January 30, 2019 from http:// racebatr.com/2017/05/04/break-letter-academia/#.

Metallic (Gopit), F. (2008). Strengthening our relation in Gespe'gewa'gi, the Seventh District of Mi'gma'gi. In L. Simpson (Ed.), *Lighting the eighth fire: The liberation, resurgence, and protection of Indigenous nations* (pp. 59–71). Winnipeg, MB: Arbeiter Ring Publishing.

Miller, J. R. (2017). *Residential schools and reconciliation: Canada confronts its history.* Toronto, ON: University of Toronto Press.

Milloy, J. (1999). A national crime: The Canadian government and the residential school system, 1879 to 1986. Winnipeg, MB: University of Manitoba Press.

National Indian Brotherhood/Assembly of First Nations. (1972). *Indian control of Indian education*. Policy paper presented to the Minister of Indian Affairs and Northern Development. Ottawa, ON: Assembly of First Nations. Retrieved January 27, 2019 from http://www.oneca.com/IndianControlofIndian Education.pdf.

Ontario Ministry of Education (2018) Release of the curriculum policy documents for: Social Studies, Grades 1–6; History and Geography, Grades 7–8 (2018); Canadian and World Studies, Grades 9–10 (2018); Cooperative Education, Grades 11–12 (2018); First Nations, Métis, and Inuit Studies; and Course Descriptions & Prerequisites Resource Document (2018). Retrieved January 27, 2019 from http://www.edu.gov.on.ca/eng/policyfunding/memos /april2018/dm-curriculum-policy-docs-course-descriptions-en.pdf.

Pete, S., Schneider, B., & O'Reilly, K. (2013). Decolonizing our practice: Indigenizing our teaching. *First Nations Perspectives, 5*(1), 99–115.

Rose, D. (1996). *Nourishing Terrains: Australian Aboriginal views of landscape and wilderness.* Canberra, AU: Australian Heritage Commission.

Royal Commission on Aboriginal People (RCAP). (1996a). *Summary. Royal Commission on Aboriginal People: Looking forward, looking back.* Retrieved January 27, 2019 from http://www.ontarioaboriginalhousing.ca/wp-content/uploads /2014/09/royal-commission-report-on-aboriginal-people.pdf.

Royal Commission on Aboriginal People (RCAP). (1996b). *Restructuring the relationship, vol. 2.* Retrieved January 27, 2019 from http://data2.archives.ca/e /e448/e011188230-02.pdf.

Sharifian, F. (2011). *Cultural conceptualizations and language: Theoretical framework and applications.* Philadelphia, PA: John Benjamins.

Shreve, B. (2015). On a dream and a prayer: The promise of world Indigenous higher education. *Tribal College Journal, 26*(3), 18–22.

Snively, G., & Williams, W. L. (Eds.) (2016). *Knowing home: Braiding Indigenous science with Western science, book 1.* Victoria, BC: University of Victoria.

Toulouse, P. (2014). Truthful narrative. *Education Canada, 54*(3), 20–25.

Truth and Reconciliation Commission (TRC) of Canada. (2012). *Truth and Reconciliation Commission of Canada: Interim report.* Winnipeg: Truth and Reconciliation Commission of Canada and Library and Archives Canada Cataloguing in Publication. Retrieved January 27, 2019 from http://www.myrobust .com/websites/trcinstitution/File/Interim%20report%20English%20 electronic.pdf.

Truth and Reconciliation Commission (TRC) of Canada. (2015). Truth and Reconciliation Commission of Canada Calls to Action. Ottawa: Government of Canada. Retrieved January 30, 2019 from https://www.aadnc-aandc.gc.ca/eng /1524494530110/1524494579700.

United Nations General Assembly. (2007). *Declaration on the Rights of Indigenous Peoples*. Paris, France: United Nations.

Williams, L. (2011). Indigenous education: Finding face, making space, having place. Retrieved January 27, 2019 from http://research.acer.edu.au/cgi/view content.cgi?article=1124&context=research_conference.

Ways of Seeing and Responding to a School in Santee Sioux Country

APRILLE PHILLIPS

This ethnographically informed case study examines the work of a state board of education (SBOE) and state department of education (SDE) engaged in the initial implementation of a state-legislated school accountability system. It chronicles the early intervention to improve a school designated as "priority" on the Santee Sioux reservation. Considering the freighted history of government intervention in American Indian education (Brayboy & Castagno, 2009; Lomawaima & McCarty, 2006), it is worth asking why students, teachers, or parents at a reservation school should trust a comprehensive state intervention and whether interventions support or subvert culturally and linguistically responsive pedagogies. This study scrutinizes how state leaders and intermediaries conceptualized the local educators and the community and whether those local educators were viewed as co-decision makers or as "objects" of mandates they had no voice in developing (Foucault, 1977).

THE GALLERY OF THE State Board of Education (SBOE) meeting room was so full that a few members of the media spilled into the adjoining hallway. They were waiting to hear how Nebraska public schools and districts had been classified in performance levels and which three schools would be named for "priority school" intervention under Nebraska's new accountability system: AQuESTT (Accountability for a Quality Education System Today and Tomorrow). Down the hallway in my Nebraska Department of Education (NDE) cubicle I watched the livestream. The announcement would be no surprise for me. In fact, I had just gotten off the phone with a superintendent, notifying him that in moments the Commissioner of Education would announce a school in his district as one of the three priority schools.

Touting the design of his first major policy implementation as Nebraska's Commissioner of Education, Dr. Matthew L. Blomstedt briefed members of the media and introduced AQuESTT as a "broader" way of thinking about accountability with the "systems of support" that would undergird intervention processes. Blomstedt then announced the three priority schools the SBOE had designated for state intervention. Not surprisingly, the schools classified in Nebraska as "needing improvement" were similar to those often identified as low-performing across the country, serving students identified as African American, Latino, Native American, or students coming from poverty (United States Commission on Civil Rights [USCCR], 2003).

As he announced each priority school, Blomstedt described a theme that each represented among schools classified in the lowest performance level. His hope, he explained, was that in selecting schools characterized by "low performance," according to themes shared by other schools, the state might learn valuable policy lessons around intervention and support that might be shared across the state. Of the three designated priority schools, one was in a working-class, mostly white, rural-community with declining enrollment; the second was in North Omaha, serving a primarily low-income African American student population; and the third was located on the Santee Sioux Reservation. Blomstedt's stated hope was that Santee Community School's (SCS) "priority school" designation would indicate that Nebraska's education policy would attend to (rather than ignore) the academic achievement of American Indian and Alaska Native children in the state.

The question-and-answer portion of the press conference hinted at the ways low-performance has become "expected" in American Indian schools. No one raised larger questions about how, in a process that singled out 87 of the state's 1,130 schools as "needing improvement," every single school on American Indian Reservation lands was classified under the lowest classification. No one asked what a state-led intervention might look like or how it might "provide a level of support" through an accountability system that leaned primarily on student performance on statewide assessments as its measuring-stick for quality. Educational challenges (and possibilities) abound in Indian Country, but it is neither straightforward nor clear that they are only or mainly challenges of accountability; and we must keep in mind that accountability systems pathologize certain kinds of schools.

This study examines how state policymakers, leaders, and intermediaries (like myself) involved throughout the implementation of Legislative Bill #438 (which came to be known as AQuESTT) saw, understood, and responded to priority school educators and members of the community at SCS. The history of government intervention in American Indian education in Santee and elsewhere raises important questions. Why should students, teachers, or parents at a reservation school trust a state intervention? How might being named a "priority school" reinforce a stigma that makes sustainable improvement more, rather than less difficult? Do intervention strategies support or subvert culturally and linguistically responsive pedagogies? Were the Santee community and school viewed throughout the process as collaborators whose voices ought to be included or as objects of school accountability policy for which they were not expected to have a voice (Foucault, 1977)?

A Brief History of American Indian Education in the Context of Santee

Brayboy, Faircloth, Lee, Maaka, and Richardson (2015) assert (and I agree) that "[i]n order to better understand and appreciate the unique educational challenges facing present-day American Indian and Alaska Native communities, it is important to understand their unique history and political relationship with the United States" (p. 2). Understanding the particular context of policymaking and implementation in the case of AQuESTT and its initial impact at SCS requires a basic knowledge of the history of the Santee and their removal to Nebraska.

Lieutenant Zebulon Pike first approached the Santee Dakota Sioux with an offer to purchase a portion of their lands in present-day Minnesota, resulting in the Sioux Treaty of 1805 and the subsequent construction of Fort Snelling in 1819. By 1854, the Santee's homeland had been confiscated through the treaties of Traverse des Sioux and Mendota and the majority of the Santee people were forcibly moved to temporary reservation lands (Bonvillain, 1996). In a final bloody uprising in 1862 led by Little Crow, 20 "Americans" were killed in an attack on the U.S. government agency in Redwood, Minnesota (Bonvillain, 1996). In response, the U.S. Government captured over 400 Santee men. Following "legal proceedings," they condemned 303 of those Santee men to death. While President Abraham Lincoln spared the lives of the majority of the men, 38 were hanged near Mankato, Minnesota the day after Christmas that same year. It remains the largest mass execution in U.S. history (Bonvillain, 1996).

The arrests, imprisonment, and multiple hangings further devastated a people already dislocated from their homelands. At this time, Hampton Denman, the Northern Superintendent of Indian Affairs encouraged the U.S. Office of Indian Affairs to permanently fix reservation lands for the tribe. He declared that "all treaties with these Indians have been abrogated, their annuities forfeited, their splendid reservation of valuable land in Minnesota confiscated by the government, their numbers sadly reduced by starvation and disease; they have been humiliated to the dust" (United States Office of Indian Affairs, 1868, p. 265). Denman asserted in his report that "wisdom and humanity" demanded the government adopt a new policy [toward the Santee] (United States Office of Indian Affairs, 1868, p. 265). He advocated that new policy should "Take them [the Santee] once more by the hand," in ways that would "restore enough of their former annuities" that members of the tribe could reestablish lives for themselves in a new home (United States Office of Indian Affairs, 1868, p. 265). The procurement of a permanent home and the enactment of this kind of policy, Denman promised, would "in a very few years," make the Santee Sioux, "good citizens and entirely self-sustaining" (United States Office of Indian Affairs, 1868, p. 266). The land in northeastern Nebraska that Denman scouted and described as "desirable" in his report became the Santee Sioux Reservation in 1869.

School as Policy Tool

Nearly 150 years before SCS was named a priority school for state intervention, another group of outsiders, white missionaries from the American Board of Missionaries, made their first attempt at "conducting school" for the Santee in the summer of 1866 (Meyer, 1993, p. 175). As has remained true since, "the primary instrument of government policy toward the Indians came to be the school" (Meyer, 1993, p. 185). Under the leadership of Alfred Riggs, the American Board of Missionaries hoped to establish "a normal academy for the training of native teachers" in Santee and in 1877 the Agent for the U.S. Office of Indian Affairs reported that the [Santee] agency was becoming a "center of education for all the Sioux" (Meyer, 1993, pp. 177–178).

When schools on the Santee Sioux Reservation opened, instruction was in the Dakota language. While it is difficult to appraise the quality or effectiveness of this schooling 150 years later, it is worth noting that the early curriculum acknowledged the history and background of the enrolled students at least to the extent that it honored and worked with their existing language. However, an order issued by Commissioner of Indian Affairs John D. C. Atkins in 1887 stated, "The instruction of the Indians in the vernacular [their native language] is not only of no use to them, but is detrimental to the cause of their education and civilization, and no school will be permitted on the reservation in which the English language is not exclusively taught" (Meyer, 1993, pp. 188–189). Riggs complied in order to maintain government financial support for the normal school (Bonvillain, 1996; Meyer, 1993) even though he pointed out in an official report submitted to the Secretary of the Interior that use of Dakota in schools on the reservation was "indispensable to the best instruction" (U.S. Department of the Interior, 1867, p. 244). Nonetheless, after 1887 instruction only in English continued in Santee.

The contract between the American Board of Missionaries and the U.S. government ended in 1893 when "the strain of trying to accommodate the school's work to the demands of the government proved disproportionate" (Meyer, 1993, pp. 188–189). Santee's schools were incorporated into Nebraska's county-based public school system. Children living in the village of Santee and across the tribe's lands attended public school districts bordering the reservation. For decades this continued, but the Santee people "yearned for their own school, which could follow a curriculum more suited to their children's needs" (santeeschools.org, 2015). The tribe finally began to realize this wish with the founding of the Santee Public School in 1971, a primary school "serving 12 students supervised by one teacher and a cook" in "one building, two double-wide trailers" (santeeschools.org, 2015). Then, with supporting funds from a federal grant, the Santee district built a brick structure and renamed itself Santee Community Schools, expanding from a K–8 school to a K–12 system.

Although the creation of a local district is rightfully celebrated, a privileging of external expertise above local knowledge has often been the case at Santee and in American Indian education at large. Outsiders acting with power and unexamined assumptions that "they know best" are well documented (Bird, Lee, & López, 2013; Hopkins, 2014; Williams & Tracz, 2016). In this spirit, SCS's designation as a priority school under Nebraska's AQuESTT can be seen as a new version of a longstanding story.

Policy Culture and Accountability Reform

Policymaking and implementation are sociocultural processes. Stein (2004) asserted that policy has often framed its beneficiaries as the "other," applying deviant or deficit frames and positioning the government (or in this case the SDE) as a "corrective force," which she described as a "policy culture" (p. 19). Applying Stein's policy culture framework "shifts the work of cultural analysis away from observation of the individuals and groups served by a policy to the interrogation of *how the policy process frames the ways we see those individuals or groups*" (Stein,

2004, p. 12, emphasis in the original). As delineated above, the history of education policy intended to serve the Santee Sioux repeatedly framed individuals as needing guidance and "correction."

The most recent national education reform policies in the United States have focused on standards, assessment, and accountability (Proefriedt, 2008). Despite stated intentions to foster the success of "every student" with focused attention on "sub-populations," in the hope of "closing achievement gaps," federal policies like No Child Left Behind (NCLB), Race to the Top, and more recently the Every Student Succeeds Act have continued to marginalize American Indian students (Balter & Grossman, 2009). These policies include assumptions about achievement that while well intended, may not be well designed to adequately support educational improvement in schools serving American Indian and Alaska Native students (Beaulieu, 2000). While it is important to acknowledge that AQuESTT is a state policy, rather than a federal one, its sweeping characterizations of entire schools and related recommendations of policy tied to those characterizations are very derivative of NCLB and the accountability movement that dominates at the federal level.

Policy approaches to improving schools in tribal communities have usually fit in two primary categories: the assimilative model and the culturally responsive model: "[While] there is no evidence that the assimilative model improves academic success, there is growing evidence that the culturally responsive model does" (Brayboy & Castagno, 2009, p. 31). Unfortunately, accountability policies include assimilationist, educational improvement, one-size-fits-all models that ignore the cultures of American Indian students and have a history of failure (Brayboy & Castagno, 2009).

A stated purpose of these assimilationist policy approaches is to advance equity, however as Lomawaima and McCarty (2006) point out, there is an inherent danger in such approaches, because "standardization in fact stratifies, segregates, and undercuts human potential, denying equality of opportunity for all" (pp. 169–170). Top-down, external improvement mandates and their associated prescriptions to "fix schools" have resulted in narrowed, less culturally responsive educational experiences for American Indian students (Castagno & Brayboy, 2008). Unfortunately, schools have placed performance on standardized tests above pedagogically sound or culturally based instruction, which not only harms Native students' academic achievement (Brayboy & Maaka, 2015; Campbell, 2007; Castagno & Brayboy, 2008; Demmert,

2001; McCarty & Lee, 2014; Nelson-Barber & Lipka, 2008) but also "compromises tribal sovereignty and Indigenous community choice" (Beaulieu, Sparks, & Alonzo, 2005, p. 4) over time.

A growing body of evidence indicates that culturally responsive models are improving outcomes for American Indian students (Brayboy & Castagno, 2009). Policy approaches responsive to cultural context affirm both language and culture as foundational to constructing knowledge (Balter & Grossman, 2009; Castagno & Brayboy, 2008; Lipka & McCarty, 1994). Intentionally and authentically incorporating local epistemologies and students' funds of knowledge goes beyond symbolic elements (e.g. words, symbols, or holidays) (Gay, 2000; Gonzales, Moll, & Amanti, 2006; Lipka & Yanez, 1998).

Just as culturally responsive pedagogy (CRP) requires educators to understand how students construct culture by drawing from both traditions and everyday lived experience (Balter & Grossman, 2009), so should educational policy culture. Stein (2004) posits that if equity is going to be advanced through educational reforms (as with AQuESTT), the policy cultures of these reforms must evolve in their commitment to equity through "purposeful work on the cultural dimensions of schooling, [that] address[es] complex considerations of students' strengths and needs" (pp. 24–25), rather than pointing to "policy beneficiaries as deviant" (Stein, 2004, p. 17). In contrast to the long history of policy implementation done to the Santee Sioux, a culturally responsive policy culture ought to forefront local voices and participation in ways that shift to culturally responsive policy cultures that incorporate new ways of seeing, understanding, constructing, and implementing.

Method

I selected an ethnographically informed approach to this case study, as policy is a social and cultural construction (Hamann & Vandeyar, 2017). I say "ethnographically informed," because while the practice-situated case study applies the tools of ethnography (such as participant observation, artifact collection, informal communications, and field notes), it does not presume the holism of an ethnography (Erickson, 1984). Bartlett and Vavrus's (2014) depiction of a vertical case study seems apt here. In brief, they point to the value of cases that link macro to micro, as in this case where federal policy currents (like accountability and naming low-performing schools) manifest in state legislative debates, SBOE directives, SDE intervention, and ultimately school-level negotiation of all of the above.

The permission I had to concurrently study and engage in this work was from my employer (the state department of education) and the review of the university IRB where I wrote my dissertation. Per the agreement I could chronicle what I saw and did and always when I was in Santee I acknowledged my twin role. Still, this pointed my dissertation (and this article) in particular directions. While I am sure there were a range of local opinions about the state intervention, my overt tie to the SDE inhibited my ability to gather those opinions. There may be an account of Santee skepticism, wariness, enthusiasm, and/or jadedness that could provide another angle on the intervention. But those possibilities are not what I was positioned to reliably chronicle. Rather, given my role, as well as my access to and familiarity with the abundant public records related to legislative debates and state meetings, the empirical account I can offer is how Santee (both community and school) were interacted with and viewed by those with decision making authority to shape the intervention.

My own role as researcher as well as employee of the SDE in Nebraska at the time of data collection means that I am not a "detached participant" (Agar, 1980). Instead, as Hamann (2003) describes, I was an "active participant" with close proximity to this inquiry in my assigned role as priority school liaison to SCS. I spent more than 200 hours in Santee and many more engaged in communication with administrators, staff, and local board members between August 2015 and January 2017, when these data were collected. Yet as Hamann and Vandeyar (2017) note, my involvement means this was "a story I could tell." This researcher posture (Wolcott, 1992) presented challenges that are likely transparent to the reader. At the time, as both employee and researcher I raised questions and shared initial critique as I was in the unique position to learn about the extant assumptions present in conversations in Santee and in board rooms among decision makers at the SDE. With the perspective of time and distance (I am no longer a representative of the state) I have a vantage point where I can see what I could not see or even articulate at the time.

While a policy insider, I am not Santee Dakota Sioux and must acknowledge, that as an outsider, particularly one who at the time of this study represented the state, I am limited by the depth and breadth of my linguistic and cultural knowledge. I owe a debt of gratitude to my colleagues and friends in Santee for sharing their perspectives and for allowing me, over time, to become more "Aprille" and less "Aprille-from-the state." However, the extent I was subject to any local scrutiny in Santee is a reminder in microcosm that the reaction to me was informed by the reaction to agents of the state who had proceeded me. While there are real limitations to how well I could or did know Santee, I was well situated to capture some of how the state conceptualized Santee, an important perspective to document. The presence of Santee voices may seem strikingly absent throughout the initial intervention chronicled here. Sadly, this is reflective of the problematic absence of Santee voices in the rooms where public policy decisions about Santee were being made. There were moments when Santee educators and community leaders were present, but almost always (locally) as recipients of the state-determined intervention or at state-level meetings where the intervention was framed as much needed aid to a low-performing school. Santee leaders were not positioned to do much more than verify resource scarcities and various social challenges in their community. Indeed, this new iteration of the longstanding pattern in American Indian education of American Indians being talked at rather than talked with (Lomawaima & McCarty, 2006) is a key thesis of this article.

Data include a range of public artifacts and reports submitted by Santee Community School and the consultant to the Nebraska State Board of Education, newsletters, and e-mail correspondence that are available thanks to Nebraska's open meeting and public records statutes (Neb. Rev. Stat. § 84–712.01 & § 84–1411), as well as my own field notes. I borrowed from the analytic tools of ethnography for the processes of data collection and analysis of documents and field notes, using an iterative process that included coding of themes and analytic memos (Bowen, 2009; Owen, 2014) facilitated through the tool MaxQDA 12 Plus, a qualitative research software.

The Study

Nearly two years before Commissioner Blomstedt's priority school press conference, in one of the last debates on the proposed legislation LB438 in Nebraska's legislature, Senator Larson, representing rural northeastern Nebraska, which included the Santee Reservation, expressed concerns about whether schools like SCS might have a chance at being selected as a priority school (Nebraska 103rd Legislature 2nd Sess., 2014). Larson explained,

> I have one of the lowest performing schools in the state in my district, Santee High School, that represents a reservation. And my concern is, is this . . . you know, they have had . . . and the school board and the local community has done a lot to try to work on that school, but there's

issues, underlying issues that continue to hinder it or hold it back. (Nebraska 103rd Legislature 2nd Sess. 2014a)

Senator Larson expressed frustration that even if named a priority school, schools might not make the necessary improvements and he pointed to what he perceived as NDE repeatedly "putting on blinders" regarding other education policy reforms that could "help" schools "like Santee," including charter schools, teacher certification, and Teach for America. In his time holding the floor, Larson questioned who might be selected to intervene and what might happen should a priority school not "turnaround." He went on to say that "there [could] still could be a school that's a priority school for five years or ten years with no conversion." In his final statements, Larson advocated that instead of implementing "something watered down" the state should consider "real education reforms" (i.e., charter schools) that "were some of the best in the nation" because "we know there's been turnarounds [in those programs]" (Nebraska 103rd Legislature 2nd Sess. 2014a). Setting aside how accurate the Senator's comments were regarding supposedly excellent charter schools that succeeded in places like Santee, at the time of his comments, Larson would have been well-aware of the recent turmoil in Santee. A month before the floor debate on the school accountability legislation, the Santee tribal police had escorted the district's superintendent off the reservation. The school was in the midst of an external evaluation of their $3.1 million School Improvement Grant (SIG) implementation and reeling from an FBI investigation into whether their superintendent had embezzled federal funds from the grant. The superintendent was eventually charged with stealing more than $314,000 in federal funds from the school (a trial following a 2017 grand jury indictment is still pending as of this writing). In fact, a year and a half and two superintendents later, following the passage of a similar bill to the one Larsen was debating on the legislative floor, SCS would be named one of the first three priority schools in the state.

Policy Mediation and Implementation Across the Street at NDE

LB438, the legislation passed by Nebraska's legislature and signed into law outlined a basic framework for a new education accountability system that, in imitation of No Child Left Behind and similar policy currents, would include the classification of all public schools and districts by performance levels and the designation of up to three priority schools for SBOE-directed intervention. Thus, it became the statutory responsibility of the SBOE to (a) determine the accountability measures used for classifying schools, (b) design a process for selecting three priority schools, and (c) develop a system of support and intervention for priority schools. Branded as a "bolder, broader, and better" accountability system, AQuESTT relied primarily on student-performance on statewide assessments (NeSA) to classify schools and districts in four performance classifications: Excellent, Great, Good, and Needs Improvement (Nebraska State Board of Education, 2015). For the first time in the state's education governance history, the SBOE was authorized to bypass local school board authority to intervene in local schools.

In my role as Student Achievement Coordinator at NDE, the Commissioner had tapped me to join an AQuESTT work-team where I was charged to develop potential models that could be used in priority school designation. And so, a couple of nights before the press conference where schools would be announced, I sat at my dining room table until the early hours of the morning looking through the short-list of schools the Commissioner was considering recommending to the SBOE for priority school designation. I knew well the stigmatizing power of a "needs improvement" designation, (Mintrop & Trujillo, 2005; Murillo & Flores, 2002).

Two days after Santee's priority school designation, Deputy Commissioner Deb Frison asked if I would act as the NDE liaison to SCS. I expressed my hesitancy. She assured me that the work in Santee would be done through authentic relationship and partnership. By the time I left her office, I was one of the outsiders headed to Santee and one month later (January 2016) I turned my car off Hwy 12 onto the Santee spur, a two-lane highway winding in and around rugged hills leading to the village of Santee.

Policy Implementation in Santee

A public school on the Santee Sioux Reservation, SCS is governed by a locally elected board, and all board members are members of the Santee Sioux tribe. Despite the SBOE's expanded authority to oversee the development and implementation of an intervention in designated priority schools under AQuESTT, the local school, district, and board, were, according to statute, expected to cooperate to ensure their continued state accreditation to operate in the state of Nebraska (Neb. Rev. Stat. §§ 79–760.06-.07).

Having been identified as a Persistently Low Achieving School (PLAS) in previous years according to federal accountability metrics (under NCLB), SCS pursued and was awarded sizable 3-year Title I School Improvement Grants (SIG) for both the elementary school ($1, 527, 551) and high school ($1,616,492) in 2010 (Holman, Welch, & Baumfalk, 2014). A formal evaluation of the SIG's impact highlighted "little change" that occurred over the course of the three-year implementation and recommended that future investments intended to improve student outcomes as well as evaluations of those programs needed to take into account the contextual factors present in each unique site (Holman et al., 2014).

Just a year after the SIG finished and the evaluation was filed, SCS had once again been identified for intervention. This was not popular news in a district whose boundaries encompass a single community with a population of about 500 people, and where nearly 40% of eligible students opted to attend school in the adjacent district (Nebraska Department of Education, 2014) because of its reputation for being the "better school" to attend. Santee's designation came just weeks after their third superintendent in three years was put on indefinite administrative leave. The only remaining administrator in the building was a first-year principal with a provisional administrative license.

I made that first visit to SCS within this context. Upon entering the community, I drove slowly through town toward the school where I parked my car and checked my phone for any last-minute messages from NDE. I took a deep breath, made a sprint through the cold, and stepped inside. Upon my entrance into the school's open atrium, I passed a large mural chronicling the resistance, hangings, forced migration, and resettlement of the Santee Sioux here to the very land upon which I stood. I felt the weight of "the state" heavy on my shoulders in this "intervention and support" capacity.

That morning, sitting among the gathered K–12 staff, the tone hardly felt positive. I found the first-year principal to be passionate about the students and community, but also struggling to hold a demoralized staff together and moving in the same direction. He introduced me to the skeptics who were all too familiar with outside "experts" and even more hesitant with an outsider from NDE.

One of the first questions a veteran teacher leader in the district asked me was, "So, what's this *really* going to look like?" She emphasized the word "really." We sat in silence for a moment. I felt my heart pounding in my head. I repeated what I had heard Commissioner Blomstedt say, that progress plans would be tailored to the needs of each of the three schools, so that lessons might be learned to better support other similar schools. "Whatever the process is," I said, "it will vary according to school." The goal was for the plan to be built in coming months through a collaborative process with NDE, the regional educational service unit (ESU), the school, and the community. I did not yet know what an "intervention" implementation might look like but I believed that a progress plan would follow a collaborative process to "diagnose" key areas to improve academic achievement. What happened in practice, however, did not match this initial vision. Collaboration cannot be mandated, but I am not convinced that it was even what AQuESTT promoters actually anticipated.

By February 2016, NDE contracted with an external consultant to support priority school intervention work. The consultant, a recently retired assistant superintendent from a mid-size district in an East Coast state was initially contracted ($18,000) to conduct a diagnostic review of each of the three priority schools (NDE, 2016a). This contract was renewed ($18,000) in June 2016 when the consultant was asked to develop priority school improvement plans for each school. Then in August the SBOE approved contracts ($256,000) that authorized the consultant to oversee the implementation of priority school progress plans in all three schools in the first year of implementation (NDE, 2016b; NDE, 2016c).

A month after my first visit as NDE's liaison to Santee, Deputy Commissioner Frison, the consultant, and a small team of NDE staff made an initial "relationship-building" visit to SCS. In a meeting that lasted fewer than 2 hours, the principal and a handful of staff sat around a table with the representatives of the state and the East Coast consultant. In the meeting, the principal reiterated the staff and community's request that the "Santee DNA" be put into whatever the progress plan or interventions might be "or it would never work." As we exited the school, I walked past that same mural with its chronicle of the history of the Santee and wondered (a bit uneasily) what lay ahead in Santee's priority school implementation.

The consultant returned to Santee a couple of weeks later and conducted priority school diagnostic reviews with representatives from NDE (myself included) in tow. The protocol encompassed a half-day visit where the consultant interviewed the principal and facilitated short conversations with students and community members using a "Glows and Grows" facilitation, and a basic examination of descriptive school data (i.e., assessment, student mobility, attendance). Despite overwhelming contextual contrasts among the three schools in terms of local histories and demographics, the consultant organized each priority school's diagnostic review, and later, action plan for improvement and implementation around what she described as her "three levers of improvement: clear and compelling direction, staff and student culture, instructional leadership capacity" (Nebraska State Board of Education, 2016). Santee's plan, like those developed for the other two schools, focused primarily on teachers improving instruction and principals improving their practice as instructional leaders (i.e., standards-aligned learning targets and instructional coaching) (Nebraska State Board of Education, 2016). The plan was produced after a site visit and some interaction, but could not accurately be described as a product of ongoing collaboration.

In July 2016, in the state capital of Lincoln, Nebraska, members of Santee's local board reviewed the consultant's priority school plan for SCS. The Santee board, their legal counsel, another superintendent (a novice on a provisional license), the principal, and a newly hired elementary principal represented Santee in a meeting that included Commissioner Blomstedt, Deputy Commissioner Frison, staff from NDE (including myself), and representatives of the ESU that serves Santee and 34 other small districts and individual schools, including several Catholic schools.

We sat around a hotel conference room table, thick binders in front of us. I thumbed down the tabs of the progress plan's "draft" watermarked pages as the Santee board president described, with great pride and emotion, what it was like to attend SCS in the 1980s. He acknowledged the challenges facing the students in his community and expressed a desire for stability in the school. His vision was a Santee where students would stop getting on a bus to attend the neighboring district and all children would feel the same pride he felt about being a graduate of a public school governed by members of the tribe. He described a place that would celebrate the Santee people and prepare the future leaders of the tribe and community for greater opportunities. I watched the tears in the eyes of other board members and blinked back my own. I thought once again of that mural in the entryway of SCS and Santee felt suddenly far away from the floor of the legislative chambers or from the pages of a progress plan before me that lacked "Santee's DNA."

In their August 2016 meeting the Nebraska SBOE reviewed and then approved the consultant's priority school plans. Each district with a priority school sent their representation to the meeting. I sat among

Santee's leadership team in the same boardroom gallery where Santee had been named a priority school less than a year before. In introducing Santee's plan, Commissioner Blomstedt told the full board,

> Santee's been through a lot, just unstable from an administrative level. I've watched that really, I mean, unfortunately my first, not even, it was the first day after I was selected, not even on the job yet here and I was in a meeting about Santee. There had been a level of discord there and problems for some time (Nebraska State Board of Education, 2016).

Blomstedt introduced the external consultant as an element that would be pivotal to building the capacity necessary to "help Santee." He explained that the consultant's contract would provide instructional leadership for the district.

A SBOE member responded to Blomstedt's comments, asking about the scope of the contract's work. He said,

> When you talk about Santee, you've got some very special issues. You got fetal alcoholism that affects a lot of the children. You got diabetes that is rampant, you know? As we go through this process, are we dealing with those issues as well in what we're doing in our plan? I mean, those are serious issues that you know, they're impacting the learning of those children in a great way. (Nebraska State Board of Education, 2016)

Both Commissioner Blomstedt and Deputy Commissioner Frison agreed that the problems in Santee went beyond building instructional capacity. Blomstedt told board members,

> When the school community isn't functioning, other things are at a detriment there as well, and so if we can get that to be a really solid base, I think you'll also see other things come along that is really remarkable. (Nebraska State Board of Education, 2016)

Blomstedt indicated that in the process of implementing Santee's progress plan, broader work could be accomplished as well. Ultimately the SBOE voted unanimously to approve Santee's first year's progress plan and to extend a contract to the external consultant to facilitate the work.

Discussion

Despite stated good intentions for the growth and learning of every child, from the legislative floor to the SBOE board room to the development of progress plans for Santee, the course of Nebraska's most recent school accountability reform effort reflects a policy culture pointing toward deficits to be corrected (Stein, 2004). More than a century after the American Board of Missionaries established a school for the Santee Sioux, the dynamics of a policy culture that invokes an external expertise (whether a mission board, state department of education, or an out-of-state consultant) to intervene, to do for, and to "fix" a school and by extension a community, seems eerily repetitive.

Seeing Santee as "Broken" and "Needing Help"

Nebraska policymakers did not ignore the academic achievement of American Indian students in the state and attempted to improve outcomes through the work at SCS. However, throughout the study of AQuESTT's policy evolution, from the legislative floor to classrooms at SCS, Santee was consistently referred to as "broken." Just as Hampton Denman (the Northern Superintendent of Indian Affairs in 1867) claimed that the U.S. government should take the Santee people "once more by the hand" in order to make them "good citizens and entirely self-sustaining" (United States Office of Indian Affairs, 1868, p. 265), so too did policymakers across the tiers of AQuESTT's development.

Proposed "help" included this notion of "good" leadership coming in to "stabilize" the school along with other recommendations for policy fixes external to Santee (i.e., charter schools, Teach for America) made on the legislative floor. With time constraints in statute for completing a progress plan to be approved by the SBOE, the time necessary for authentic relationship building and then a partnership to collaboratively develop a progress plan was skipped. The policy prescription determined by NDE and the SBOE was to externally contract expertise with a consultant, incorporating little local voice in the final progress plan submitted to the SBOE. Regardless of the distinct "challenges" or "barriers to student achievement" that each priority school faced, there was a common solution: the consultant's "three levers of improvement." Thus, in two days a month in each school, the consultant would "support" principals in coaching teachers to better align instruction to state standards (i.e., posted learning targets, curriculum scope and sequence, new instructional materials). The only way to "get out of priority school status," the consultant explained (with some accuracy), was to improve scores on the annual statewide assessment.

The focus on boosting student achievement as measured by a standardized assessment had similar consequences to what Balter and Grossman (2009) found as a result of a similar emphasis following No Child Left Behind in the Navajo community. Under AQuESTT, time to attend to culturally responsive ways of teaching was limited and the adherence to teaching the "necessary skills at the appropriate depth of knowledge" did not incorporate local cultural knowledge or local educator expertise (although the local administrators and a handful of teachers attempted to maintain and strengthen culturally responsive pedagogies). By and large, the policy prescription applied to the three priority schools ignored each site's local culture, history, and knowledge resources and left unexamined how apt state standards were as a measure for what these students brought to school or needed. This is problematic for two key reasons: (a) Viewing academic performance among the Santee as the same as other "underrepresented minority" groups (like those attending other priority schools in Nebraska) "ignores and undermines the totality of history and driving concepts like self-governance, sovereignty, and self-determination" (Brayboy et al., 2015, p. 5). (b) In this case, just as in the examples of policy prescriptions outlined throughout the Santee Sioux's history, local educators and the community were not viewed as co-decision makers; instead, they became objects of mandates they had only limited voice in developing (Foucault, 1977).

Culturally Responsive Policy Cultures: Another Way to See Santee

And yet there is a contrasting way to think about work to improve learning experiences for American Indian children in the United States that begins with viewing Native knowledge and culture as "an ally" (Lomawaima & McCarty, 2006, p. 170). Stein (2004) in her critique of the assumptions embedded in the Elementary and Secondary Education Act from its creation asserted that overcoming a policy culture founded on fixing deficiencies requires an authentic commitment to equity. Cultivating a policy culture that resists "policy as "corrective force" will require deliberate and intentional work that considers local context and "invites the voice of the school in actively pursuing policy that address complex considerations of students' strengths and needs" (Stein, 2004, 24–25).

Education policymaking and implementation (and in this case stateled) intervention in schools serving Native students and communities ought to support culturally responsive practices reflecting context and voice (Beaulieu, 2006; Castagno & Brayboy, 2008; Lipka & McCarty, 1994). Crafting culturally responsive policy that attends to local context and voice requires policymakers and educational institutions to see differently, with a clearer understanding of the history and sovereignty of Indigenous peoples and their responsibility toward students and the local tribal community (Austin, 2005). The success of Montana's Indian Education for All, which has been well documented (Carjuzaa, Baldwin, & Munson, 2015; Ngai & Koehn, 2016), and Nevada's recent Native Youth Community Project grant funded by the U.S. Department of Education (Nevada Department of Education, 2017) are both examples of SDEs demonstrating culturally responsive policymaking as they work in collaboration with local tribes to support students' success academically and culturally.

It should not be surprising that external, one-size-fits-all interventions do not help schools improve students' (or educators') educational experiences, which was once again found to be true in the initial state-directed intervention at SCS. NDE did not put a formal evaluation plan in place to assess the consultant's intervention. The state relied on initial data from statewide assessments following the first year of state intervention in Santee, which were inconclusive. Due to the small number of students in the school, the modest fluctuations (both up and down) in assessed areas did not demonstrate any sort of significant change (Nebraska Department of Education, 2015). The data I collected from informal interviews and observations, however, demonstrated leaders' and educators' frustration at the narrow focus on standards-aligned instruction and assessment gains and the setting aside of what the principal described as the "Santee DNA" (i.e., Santee ways of knowing). The findings here reaffirm Demmert's (2001) conclusion that "congruency between the school environment and the language and culture of the community is critical to the success of formal learning" (p. 9), which seems like common sense but is not common practice.

Future inquiry ought to consider ways to expand the lenses through which systems can (a) recognize nuances that exist in contexts like the case of SCS, (b) provide a fresh perspective to inform how the system sees and responds to students' circumstances, and (c) act in ways that reflect culturally responsive policy and practice. Despite good intentions, the necessity of a shift toward culturally responsive policymaking became evident in Nebraska's priority school-work in Santee. Across the tiers of the system, from the legislative floor to the classroom, individuals stated their hopes for what priority school intervention might accomplish. Santee's local board president described a vision for a school that would celebrate the tribe's history and prepare its future leaders, a vision that will not happen until policymakers begin with how they listen, see, and understand.

Aprille Phillips is assistant professor of education at Southern Oregon University. Her areas of inquiry include education policy implementation along the policy-to-practice continuum, intersections of democracy and education, and the influence of transnational student mobility on identity formation.

REFERENCES

Agar, M. (1980). *The professional stranger.* Bingley, UK: Emerald Group Publishing.

Austin, R. D. (2005). Perspectives of American Indian nation parents and leaders. *New Directions for Student Services, 109,* 41–48.

Balter, A., & Grossman, F. D. (2009). The effects of the No Child Left Behind Act on language and culture education in Navajo public schools. *Journal of American Indian Education, 48*(3), 19–46.

Bartlett, L., & Vavrus, F. (2014). Traversing the vertical case study: A methodological approach to studies of educational policy as practice. *Anthropology and Education Quarterly, 45*(2), 131–147.

Beaulieu, D. L. (2000). Comprehensive reform and American Indian education. *Journal of American Indian Education, 39*(2), 29–38.

Beaulieu, D. L. (2006). A survey and assessment of culturally based education programs for Native American students in the United States. *Journal of American Indian Education, 45*(2), 50–61.

Beaulieu, D. L., Sparks, S., & Alonzo, M. (2005). Preliminary report on No Child Left Behind in Indian country. Washington, DC: National Indian Education Association.Bird, C. P., Lee, T. S., & López, N. (2013). Leadership and accountability in American Indian education: Voices from New Mexico. *American Journal of Education, 119*(4), 539–564.

Bonvillain, N. (1996). *The Santee Sioux.* Langhorne, PA: Chelsea House Publishers.

Bowen, G. A. (2009). Document analysis as qualitative research method. *Qualitative Research Journal, 9*(2), 27–40.

Brayboy, B. M. J., & Castagno, A. E. (2009). Self-determination through self-education: Culturally responsive schooling for Indigenous students in the USA. *Teaching Education, 20*(1), 31–53.

Brayboy, B., Faircloth, S. Lee, T., Maaka, M., & Richardson, T. (2015). Sovereignty and education: An overview of the unique nature of Indigenous education. *Journal of American Indian Education, 54*(1), 1–9.

Brayboy, B. M. J., & Maaka, M. J. (2015). K–12 achievement for Indigenous students. *Journal of American Indian Education, 54*(1), 63–98.

Campbell, A. E. (2007). Retaining American Indian/Alaskan Native students in higher education: A case study of one partnership between the Tohono

O'odham Nation and Pima Community College, Tucson, AZ. *Journal of American Indian Education, 46*(2), 19–41.

Carjuzaa, J., Baldwin, A. E., & Munson, M. (2015). Making the dream real: Montana's Indian education for all initiative thrives in a national climate of anti-ethnic studies. *Multicultural Perspectives, 17*(4), 198–206.

Castagno, A. E., & Brayboy, B. M. J. (2008). Culturally responsive schooling for Indigenous youth: A review of the literature. *Review of Educational Research, 78*(4), 941–993.

Demmert, W. (2001). Improving schools' academic performance among Native American students: A review of the research literature. Charleston, WV: ERIC Clearinghouse on Rural Education and Small Schools.

Erickson, F. (1984/1973). What makes school ethnography "ethnographic"? *Anthropology and Education Quarterly 15*, 51–66.

Foucault, M. (1977). *Discipline and punish.* New York, NY: Vintage Books.

Gay, G. (2000). *Culturally responsive teaching: Theory, practice and research.* New York, NY: Teachers College Press.

González, N., Moll, L. C., & Amanti, C. (Eds.). (2006). *Funds of knowledge: Theorizing practices in households, communities, and classrooms.* New York, NY: Routledge.

Hamann, E. T. (2003). Imagining the future of anthropology if we take Laura Nader seriously. *Anthropology & Education Quarterly, 34*(4), 438–449.

Hamann, E. T. & Vandeyar, T. (2017). What does an anthropologist of educational policy do? Methodological considerations. In A.E. Castagno & T.L. McCarty (Eds.). *The anthropology of education policy: Ethnographic inquiries into policy as sociocultural process* (pp. 56–74). New York, NY: Routledge.

Holman, S., Welch, G. W., & Baumfalk, B. (2014). *Evaluating the impact of Nebraska's school improvement grants.* Lincoln, NE: University of Nebraska-Lincoln, College of Education and Human Sciences.

Hopkins, T. R. (2014). Reports From the Field: American Indian self-determination in education and the Department of Interior. *Journal of American Indian Education, 53*(1), 54–60.

Lipka, J., & McCarty, T. L. (1994). Changing the culture of schooling: Navajo and Yup'ik cases. *Anthropology and Education Quarterly, 25*(3), 266–284.

Lipka, J., & Yanez, E. (1998). Identifying and understanding cultural differences: Toward culturally based pedagogy. In J. Lipka, G. Mohatt, & the Ciulistet Group (Eds.), *Transforming the culture of schools: Yup'ik Eskimo examples* (pp. 111–137). Mahwah, NJ: Lawrence Erlbaum.

Lomawaima, K. T., & McCarty, T. L. (2006). *"To remain an Indian": Lessons in democracy from a century of Native American education.* New York, NY: Teachers College Press.

McCarty, T. L., & Lee, T. S. (2014). Critical culturally sustaining/revitalizing pedagogy and Indigenous education sovereignty. *Harvard Educational Review, 84*(1), 101–124.

Meetings of public body; notice; contents; when available; right to modify; duties concerning notice; videoconferencing or telephone conferencing authorized; emergency meeting without notice; appearance before public body. Nebraska Revised Statute § 84–1411.

Meyer, R. W. (1993). *History of the Santee Sioux: United States Indian policy on trial.* Lincoln, NE: University of Nebraska Press.

Mintrop, H., & Trujillo, T. (2005). Corrective action in low performing schools: Lessons for NCLB implementation from first-generation accountability systems. *Education and Policy Analysis Archives, 13*(48), 1–30.

Murillo, Jr., E. G., & Flores, S. Y. (2002). Reform by shame: Managing the stigma of labels in high stakes testing. *The Journal of Educational Foundations, 16*(2), 93.

Nebraska 103rd Legislature 2nd Sess. (2014). *Quality education and accountability act, LB438: Floor debate.* Lincoln, NE: State of Nebraska.

Nebraska Department of Education (2014). Mobility data.

Nebraska Department of Education (2015). *Santee Community School, Statewide report card.*

Nebraska Department of Education (2016a, March 3). Contract.

Nebraska Department of Education (2016b, June 2). Contract.

Nebraska Department of Education (2016c, August 4). Contract

Nebraska State Board of Education. (2015). *December state board of education business meeting.* Lincoln, NE: State of Nebraska.

Nebraska State Board of Education. (2016). *August state board of education business meeting.* Lincoln, NE: State of Nebraska.

Nelson-Barber, S., & Lipka, J. (2008). Rethinking the case for culture-based curriculum: Conditions that support improved mathematics performance in diverse classrooms. In M. Brisk (Ed.). *Language, curriculum and community in teacher preparation* (pp. 99–123). Mahwah, NJ: Lawrence Erlbaum.

Nevada Department of Education. (2017). *Nevada only state to receive $3.251 million* U.S. Press Release, *Department of Education Native Youth Community Projects Grant.*

Ngai, P. B., & Koehn, P. H. (2016). Teacher/family partnerships for student learning: Lessons from Indian Education for All in Montana. *Journal of American Indian Education, 55*(1), 23–48.

Owen, G. T. (2014). Qualitative methods in higher education policy analysis. *The qualitative report, 19*(52), 1–19.

Proefriedt, W. (2008). *High expectations.* New York, NY: Teachers College Press.

Public records; right of citizens; full access; fee authorized. Nebraska Revised Statute § 84-712.01.

Santeeschools.org. (2015). *Santee community schools.* Available at https://www .santeeschools.org/.

Stein, S. J. (2004). *The culture of education policy.* New York, NY: Teachers College Press.

United States Commission on Civil Rights (USCCR). (2003). *A quiet crisis: Federal funding and unmet needs in Indian country.* Washington, DC: U.S. Government Printing Office.

United States Office of Indian Affairs. (1868). *Annual report of the Commissioner of Indian Affairs to the Secretary of the Interior for the fiscal year ended in 1877.* Washington, DC: U.S. Government Printing Office.

United States Office of the Interior (1867). *Annual report of the Department of the Interior: Volume 2 for the fiscal year ended in 1877.* Washington DC: U.S. Government Printing Office.

Williams, T., & Tracz, S. M. (2016). Taking back the fire: schooling experiences of Central California Indian people across generations. *Journal of American Indian Education, 55*(2), 75–98.

Wolcott, H. F. (1992). Posturing in qualitative inquiry. In M. D. LeCompte, W.L. Millroy, & J. Preissle (Eds.), *The handbook of qualitative research in education* (pp. 3–52). San Diego, CA: Academic.

Improving Kindergarten and Grade One Indigenous Students' On-Task Behavior With the Use of Movement Integration

SERENE KERPAN, M. LOUISE HUMBERT, CAROL D.
RODGERS, AND ALEXANDRA L. STODDART

The purpose of this study was to examine the effect of movement integration on the on-task behavior, a facet of self-regulation, of Indigenous kindergarten and grade one participants at an on-reserve school in Canada. Movement integration is defined as opportunities that allow for increased physical activity among children during classroom time. Methods: This study utilized participatory action research methodology. Nine ($n = 9$) kindergarten and grade one Indigenous students participated in this study. The repeated measures design used had a within subjects factor with four levels. For one-week participants' on-task behavior was measured without the use of movement integration during class time. For the subsequent two weeks on-task behavior was measured during class at two time points, before movement integration and after movement integration. Results: A two way [time (pre-lesson vs. post-lesson) x period (active lesson vs. non-active lesson)] repeated measures ANOVA revealed a significant time x period interaction [$F(1, 8) = 36.77$, $p < .001$, Partial $\eta2 = 0.821$], indicating that the movement integration intervention was effective in improving on-task behavior for the participants. Conclusion: Incorporating movement integration may be an effective way to improve the on-task behaviors of children in their first years of elementary school.

EARLY CHILDHOOD LEARNERS, who are in pre-school or their first years of elementary school, are rich in opportunity and at a critical time period for learning (Niles, Byers, & Krueger, 2007; Preston, Cottrell, Pelletier, & Pearce, 2012; White & Peters, 2013). Early learning experiences for Indigenous children hold educational, social, health, and economic potential (Faircloth, 2015; Preston et al., 2012). The delivery of quality early childhood education is a crucial tool in achieving parity between Indigenous and non-Indigenous learners because early education lays the foundation for high school and college education (Brayboy & Maaka, 2015; Niles et al., 2007). For this reason, there has been a widespread call to support the academic success of early Indigenous learners.

There is not one specific best-practice approach for supporting early childhood learning in Indigenous communities. The success of early childhood education depends on community specific cultural beliefs and behaviors and how they are integrated into the school and curriculum (Romero-Little, 2010). Up until fairly recently, dominant non-Indigenous beliefs and desired behaviors were the most often used building blocks for early education, including early education for Indigenous children (Niles et al., 2007). However, it is now recognized that pedagogical practices should be built upon the practices and beliefs of the people for whom they are designed, specifically Indigenous children (Battiste, 1998). In order for this to happen communities must identify their worldviews and their beliefs about education and children; this includes how, when, and why children learn (Romero-Little, 2010). Successful early education must also be developed for Indigenous children with the consideration of what roles they may fulfil in their Indigenous community and the larger global community, this provides them the skills to make autonomous decisions about how they want to live their lives and contribute to society (Canadian Council on Learning, 2009; Romero-Little, 2010).

There is a rich diversity in the worldviews of Indigenous communities both globally, and tribally in North America. Notwithstanding, some broad beliefs and behaviors are common among many Indigenous groups (Sarche & Whitesell, 2012). Based on these commonalities, some pedagogical values are shared across Indigenous communities. Indigenous pedagogy is often based on experiential learning (Battiste, 2002; Cajete, 2005; Castagno & Brayboy, 2008). Activities such as storytelling, discussion, cooperative learning, and reflection are often embedded in Indigenous learning (Preston et al., 2012). These approaches develop characteristics crucial to lifelong learning such as independence, self-reliance, social cooperation, and discovery (Cajete, 2005). Indigenous pedagogy brings together Indigenous values and knowledge in a holistic and flexible manner (Battiste, 2002; Cajete, 2005). These Indigenous pedagogical values can stand in contrast to traditional Euro-Western pedagogy. Teachers, in a Euro-Western fashion, might present discrete subjects in distinct time frames, utilize sedentary didactic instruction, have limited time allotted to social or cooperative learning, and use an educator-centered framework (Preston et al., 2012). However, these practices are rapidly changing in North American education systems, with holistic and diverse pedagogical approaches that complement Indigenous pedagogy being incorporated into curricula.

Given that there can be differences in pedagogical values, which are determined by distinctive cultural beliefs and behaviors, educational practices for Indigenous children need to be developed that recognize the importance of giving Indigenous communities control over early education (Preston et al., 2012). Cultural compatibility theory is a suitable theoretical model, as it is based on Indigenous communities having command over the design and implementation of early education that considers contextual realities such as community-based epistemological beliefs (Niles et al., 2007). Cultural compatibility theory aligns with the proclamations of numerous Indigenous early education scholars who identify the need to integrate culture as a key aspect of Indigenous child development and the need for educational self-determination (Cajete, 2005; Castagno & Brayboy, 2008; Sarche & Whitesell, 2012; Spicer et al., 2012).

Early Childhood Developmental Research With Indigenous Communities

Research with Indigenous Peoples on early childhood development is scant compared to the research available for non-Indigenous populations (Henrich, Heine, & Norenzayan, 2010; Marks & Coll, 2007). Moreover, the cultural context of child development, including how culture can influence developmental outcomes, has been largely ignored in the past (Sarche & Whitesell, 2012). The available evidence accumulated from research with Indigenous communities indicates that culture impacts many facets of early childhood development including cognitive development, identity, school readiness, and motivation (Marks & Coll, 2007; Spicer et al., 2012). When culture is ignored in the investigation and promotion of child development little headway is made in supporting Indigenous child development (Spicer et al., 2012).

True partnership between Indigenous communities and early childhood researchers needs to be fostered in order to fully bring culture into early childhood research. Approaches such as community-based participatory research supports research that starts with an understanding of community-based values, beliefs, and behaviors. When this knowledge forms the foundation of childhood developmental research the cultural contexts in which children live can be integrated into the research questions and methods, reducing the risk of perpetuating the problems of previous research on Indigenous child development (Spicer et al., 2012).

Indigenous communities have long known the crucial importance of culture in child development and have advocated for culture informing child development interventions; in recent years researchers and others in positions which impact child development in Indigenous communities have become responsive to this need (Castagno & Brayboy, 2008; Niles et al., 2007; Preston et al., 2012; Spicer et al., 2012). The implementation of childhood developmental interventions that consider and integrate culture will increase the quantity of evidence necessary to demonstrate the value of implementing culturally based interventions (Sarche & Whitesell, 2012). However, research needs to be methodologically rigorous if it is to impact decision making (Spicer et al., 2012).

School Entry and Self-Regulation

The first years of elementary school are a time of change for early learners. Whether a child is Indigenous or non-Indigenous, new behavioral expectations are introduced (Marks & Coll, 2007; Rimm-Kaufman, Curby, Grimm, Nathanson, & Brock, 2009). As children leave pre-school or the home environment, the goals, demands, and types of evaluations placed upon them change (Rimm-Kaufman, Pianta, & Cox, 2000). One crucial behavior for children entering school is self-regulation. Self-regulation encompasses a child's ability to manage their emotions, focus their attention, and inhibit some behaviors while exhibiting others (Blair & Razza, 2007). Self-regulation is linked to numerous positive outcomes for early learners, such as academic success and social development (Blair, 2002; Wagner et al., 2017). For early learners self-regulation looks different in different situations; sometimes it might be sitting and listening, while at other times it might apply in an active learning situation, or in a cooperative or social learning setting. Helping children in their first years of elementary school to self-regulate behavior lays the foundation for its continuation throughout their school years (McClelland & Cameron, 2011). Available research demonstrates that self-regulation provides a foundation for academic achievement from pre-school through adulthood (McClelland & Cameron, 2011).

Self-regulation is best described as a Euro-Western construct, and the large majority of research investigating self-regulation has been done with Western, Educated, Industrialized, Rich and Democratic (WEIRD) populations (Henrich et al., 2010). A recent review examining different cultural variations of children's development of self-regulation found that many of the behaviors that make up self-regulation—such as attention and compliance—are influenced by cultural values and norms

(LeCuyer & Zhang, 2015). Thus, it is important to work with Indigenous communities to understand what importance self-regulation has for their children based on cultural values (LeCuyer & Zhang, 2015). For example, a 2017 study examined a self-regulation intervention with Australian Aboriginal children (Wagner et al., 2017). The study reported here took a similar approach to determine if self-regulation was an acceptable outcome and fit with the values and needs of the community. Through a participatory action research approach the community partners on this project determined that self-regulation was a relevant behavior to examine because it fit with their community-specific pedagogical values. Community partners articulated that whether a child is learning math, science, or language from either pedagogical worldview (Indigenous or Euro-Western) they need to be able to exhibit self-regulation to learn.

Self-Regulation and Physical Activity

One strategy to help children adjust to school and self-regulate is to increase opportunities for them to be physically active (Becker, McClelland, Loprinzi, & Trost, 2014; Carson et al., 2016; Schmidt et al., 2017). Research over the past decade has shown that physical activity improves children's academic achievement and learning abilities (de Greeff, Bosker, Oosterlaan, Visscher, & Hartman, 2018). More specifically, numerous studies have shown that physical activity improves on-task behavior for elementary school children (Carlson et al., 2015; Castelli et al., 2014; Grieco, Jowers, & Bartholomew, 2009; Harvey et al., 2018; Ma, Mare, & Gurd, 2014; Mahar et al., 2006; Riley, Lubans, Morgan, & Young, 2015; Szabo-Reed et al., 2017). On-task behavior at school can be described as "behavior that follows the class rules and is appropriate to the learning situation" (Mahar et al., 2006) and "actively or passively attending to the assigned work" (Shapiro, 2011). On-task behavior is a key indicator of self-regulation as it requires children to manage their behavior and attention, compelling them to inhibit and exhibit certain behaviors based on the task at hand.

To our knowledge there has been no published work examining how physical activity effects self-regulation or on-task behavior for Indigenous children generally or for kindergarten or grade one children specifically. Additionally, little published research focuses on the incorporation of Indigenous values and beliefs in physical education or school-based physical activity in general (Robinson, Borden, & Robinson, 2012).

Movement Integration

One way to increase daily physical activity for early learners is to provide movement integration (MI). MI is defined as opportunities that allow for reduced sedentariness and/or increased physical activity, at any level of intensity, among children during classroom time (Webster, Russ, Vazou, Goh, & Erwin, 2015). MI can involve activity that is done solely to increase physical activity time or it may involve physical activity with curriculum integrated into the activity (e.g., math activities that involve movement). Multiple positive outcomes can occur from MI, including an increase in daily physical activity, reinforcement of academic content, improved learning outcomes, and preservation of time allotted to academic instruction (Webster et al., 2015).

MI has been used successfully in studies examining how physical activity affects on-task behavior in grades two through six (Carlson et al., 2015; Grieco et al., 2009; Ma et al., 2014; Mahar et al., 2006; Riley et al., 2015). Only one study has examined a similar type of MI with pre-school children; results indicate that the pre-school children who experienced MI had better early literacy skills (Kirk, Vizcarra, Looney, & Kirk, 2014).

Although research is emerging on MI with both pre-school children and older elementary school children, no published research examines if such a strategy is successful with children in kindergarten and grade one. Nor does any published research examine the impact of MI on on-task behavior for Indigenous students. Because the fundamental tenets of MI align with Indigenous pedagogy, emphasizing learning through experience and movement (Battiste, 2002; Castagno & Brayboy, 2008; Cajete, 2005), exploring the intersect of Indigenous pedagogy and MI is a worthy undertaking.

The purpose of this study was to collaborate with Indigenous school partners to examine the effects of MI on the on-task behavior of Indigenous students entering elementary school.

Method

Participants

"Indigenous Peoples" is an inclusive term that globally represents descendants of those who inhabited a geographical region prior to colonization (First Peoples Worldwide, 2016). In Canada, Indigenous Peoples are known as Aboriginal Peoples in the Canadian Constitution. Aboriginal Peoples are represented by three groups: First Nations, Métis, and

Inuit (Constitution Act of Canada, 1982). Differences among Aboriginal Peoples in Canada are related to ethnicity (First Nations, Métis, Inuit, and those with or without registered treaty status), geography (remote, rural, on-reserve, urban), and jurisdiction (federal, provincial, tribe, band) (Smylie & Anderson, 2006). A rich diversity of social, economic, political, and environmental circumstances form important variances among Aboriginal communities (Waldram, Herring, & Young, 2006).

We use the term Indigenous to refer to all Aboriginal groups in Canada. To refer to a certain group, as defined by the Canadian Constitution, or to research pertaining solely to that group, then we use that group's name. When describing the community that took part in this study the appropriate term of First Nation will be used.

This study was conducted in collaboration with a First Nation elementary school located in an on-reserve First Nation community. The community is within a half an hour drive to a mid-sized Canadian prairie city and has less than 1,000 community members. The elementary school has less than 100 students and uses provincial Ministry of Education curriculum, which includes language arts, health education, art, science, mathematics, physical education, and science curriculum for early learners. The early years Ministry curriculum is holistic in that it supports learning through discovery, creativity, play, and relationships. Also, the Ministry of Education encourages the use of Indigenous pedagogy and the integration of Indigenous knowledge and language in all provincial schools. The school-day schedule at the school where the study took place is divided into 45-minute periods, but within these periods numerous learning activities can take place. This was often the case in the early learners' classrooms, where it was unrealistic to have small children attend to one single task for 45 minutes. Often a curricular topic or theme was covered in the 45 minutes through different pedagogical strategies. The nine participants ($n = 9$) in this study were in a kindergarten and grade one combined class. The teacher of the grade one and kindergarten class was a First Nation woman who was early in her teaching career.

The power calculation used to establish sample size was done with G Power 3.1 (Faul, Erdfelder, Buchner, & Lang, 2009). Using α of 0.05 at 80% power, it was predicted that six participants were needed for this study. The repeated measures design (discussed in succeeding section) used in this study had a within subjects' factor with four levels. This design increases the statistical power for detecting change in a smaller sample size because it allows for the assessment of within changes over time through multiple measures (Guo, Logan, Glueck, &

Muller, 2013). It should be noted that the entire class of 14 students took part in the intervention activities, which the teacher designated as a teaching method and curricular implementation. However only the nine participants and their parents or guardians who gave informed consent and assent took part in the measurement component (64% participation rate). Ethical approval for this study was acquired from the researcher's university ethics board and from the participating school's First Nation Council.

Participatory Action Research

Participatory action research (PAR) is community-engaged research that shares power with and engages community partners in a research process that aims to enact change, action, and reflection (Baum, MacDougall, & Smith, 2006; Israel, Eng, Schulz, & Parker, 2005). We chose a PAR approach to conduct research in conjunction with an Indigenous school and community. When researching with Indigenous peoples, an approach that promotes relationships, collaboration, long-term engagement, and mutual benefits is ethical and culturally appropriate (Canadian Institutes of Health Research, Natural Sciences and Engineering Research Council of Canada, & The Social Sciences and Humanities Research Council of Canada, 2014). Relationships are crucial to engage in meaningful research, for both schools and Indigenous communities (Allen, Mohatt, Markstrom, Byers, & Novins, 2012). In schools, relationships are often formed among all types of school members including administration, teachers, and students. These diverse relationships allow for a rich understanding of the setting and a well-informed project (McHugh, Kingsley, & Coppola, 2013; Oosman, Smylie, Humbert, & Henry, 2016). Relationship-building as a research process is crucial to conducting decolonizing research (Wilson, 2001).

The study presented here was part of a larger PAR project that included one qualitative and two quantitative studies. The two quantitative interventions were developed and implemented with the community as the change and action aspects of the PAR model, while the qualitative study was the reflective and re-planning phase of PAR (Kerpan, Humbert, Abonyi, 2019).

Prior to starting the research process, Kerpan, the lead researcher, volunteered at the school. She continued to volunteer during and after completion of the study. Volunteering fostered relationship-building at the school. Spending her days as a member of the school community provided hundreds of moments to foster friendships within the walls of the staff room, kitchen, gymnasium, and classrooms. Conducting research with Indigenous peoples must begin with strong reciprocal relationships in place (Allen et al., 2012; Castellano, 2004). These relationships help to mitigate the potential for stereotyping and misinterpretation of results, which have historically been issues in research with Indigenous communities (Canadian Institutes of Health Research et al., 2014; Castellano, 2004).

School leaders, teachers, and researchers worked together to develop and conduct this study. The partnership and decision-making processes were founded on the belief that all involved had valuable knowledge to contribute. Respecting everyone's knowledge was key in balancing power and overcoming the professional dominance that can occur in community-based research (Baum et al., 2006). Collaboration occurred through community planning meetings, daily school leadership and teacher meetings, and the use of a community research agreement. Decisions and conversations were documented in field notes and email communications.

From the earliest stage of deciding what outcome to measure, what ages should be involved, and what intervention should be utilized, to the final stages of deciding how to disseminate findings a team approach to decision making was used. In early meetings the researcher presented a variety of cognitive outcomes associated with physical activity as possible outcomes to investigate, but was also careful to ensure that these outcomes were not the only options. She asked if there were values or behaviors that were culturally specific to the community that could be explored. Community members expressed that they wanted their students to learn about language and traditional practices, but much of this was already being integrated into the school landscape. For them, having students who were in school and ready to learn was an important outcome that would facilitate the children learning about their culture. From there, the conversations quickly focused on self-regulation and children being on-task as important outcomes. Many people agreed that self-regulation and being on-task were crucial for all types of learning and crossed cultural confines. Whether children were going to be on the land learning to hunt, or at a desk learning mathematics, they needed to be able to manage their behavior and focus attention.

Subsequent research partnerships with the community were developed after this study, an important aspect of long-term engagement. Mutual benefits were realized through opportunities for teacher professional development, visits by a trained professional who helped implement an education intervention, and access to university resources such as field trips to the researcher's university physical activity complex. The researcher benefited through education attainment and career growth.

Design

This study used a two-way, [time (pre lesson vs post lesson) x period (active lesson vs non-active lesson)] repeated measures design (see Figure 1). For a one-week period usual practice data was collected. This was called the non-active lesson period (NALP) because the students received no additional physical activity during class time. During this week the kindergarten/grade one teacher taught her class as usual throughout the day so that data could be collected on how on-task the participants were under regular circumstances. On-task data was collected in a mid-morning lesson and mid-afternoon lesson. Both lessons were 45 minutes in length; these lessons will be referred to as the "non-active" lessons. During the non-active lessons the on-task data was collected at the beginning of the lesson and at the end of the lesson (pre-lesson and post-lesson) in order to assess any trend in the ability to stay on-task throughout a lesson.

The one-week NALP was followed by a two-week "active lesson" period (ALP). The active lessons (ALP) were taught at the same time of day, covered the same academic subject, and were the same length in time as the non—active lessons (NALP). In the middle of the active lesson (approximately 25 minutes after the start of the class) the students participated in a five-minute physical activity game that incorporated

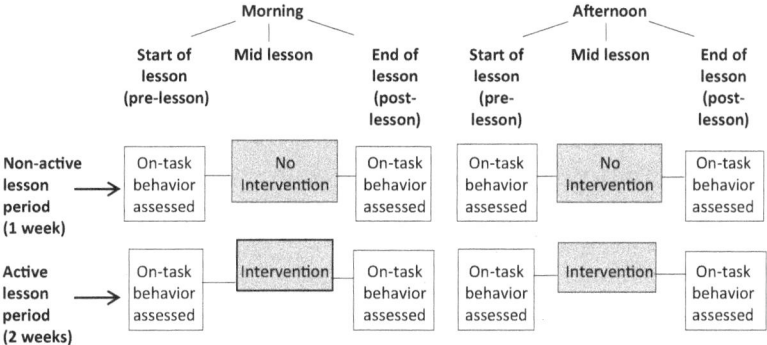

Figure 1. Study design.

curricular content relevant to the lesson. During these active lessons the same measurements of on-task ability were taken as in the non-active lesson to determine how the MI affected the participants' abilities to stay on-task.

Intervention

The MI lessons were adapted from the *Energizers* activities developed by the Activity Promotion Laboratory in the Department of Exercise and Sport Science at East Carolina University (Mahar et al., 2010). The *Energizers* team developed a series of in-class physical activities for grades 3–5 and K-2 that integrate academic concepts fundamental to curricula in both the United States and Canada. These activities are available at http://www.ecu.edu/cs-hhp/exss/apl-projects.cfm. Previous research has shown that *Energizers* are effective at improving the on-task ability of children in grades four and five (Mahar et al., 2006).

A combination of factors led to the choice to use *Energizers*. The primary consideration was that *Energizers* was one of the only MI programs widely available at the time of study design that had been proven to improve on-task behavior. Also, given the emergent and collaborative nature of this PAR study, which required many hours of collaborative development, the academic advisory committee supporting this research suggested a validated intervention would make more manageable the amount of time and effort necessary for study design. The choice of *Energizers* impacts interpretation of this research. Although the research process was collaborative in all aspects of decision-making, the intervention games and activities lacked any Indigenous knowledge, language, or symbols. This limitation is more fully examined in the discussion section.

In the morning before school started, the researcher and teacher picked out the *Energizer* activities for that day to ensure the *Energizers* content reflected the lesson's content. An example of an *Energizers* used in the intervention is a game called *Pass it on*. *Pass it on* uses four cards of different colors. The activity leader explains to the students that each color corresponds to an activity; for example, green means swim, or yellow means twist. The students each get a card and does that activity for 15 seconds; then the leader says "pass it on" and the student passes their card to another student. They determine the color of the new card, recall what activity is associated with the card, and perform that activity for another 15 seconds. The game continues for five minutes.

Defining and Measuring On-Task Behavior

Two observers assessed on-task behavior through direct observation. Because of the challenging nature of measuring on-task behavior Mahar (2011) established guidelines for collecting credible on-task data: (a) accurately define the behavior so it can be measured reliably, (b) train observers to be objective and nonjudgmental, (c) ensure inter-observer reliability prior to field research, and (d) ensure inter-observer reliability in the research data. We followed these guidelines, using definitions for on- and off-task behavior developed in previous research (Grieco et al., 2009; Mahar et al., 2006; Shapiro, 2011). The six categories measured were: on-task motor, on-task verbal, on-task passive, off-task motor, off-task verbal, and off-task passive. Figure 2 provides definitions and examples of these six coding categories.

Researchers measured on-task behavior for 15 minutes at the beginning of class (pre-lesson) and then again for 15 minutes at the end of class (post-lesson). Fifteen minutes was selected because of the length of time dedicated to subjects and because a similar previous study has used a 15-minute measurement intervals (Grieco et al., 2009). During observations, momentary time sampling was used to collect the on-task data. In momentary time sampling, observers recorded what happened at a predetermined moment (Hintze, Volpe, & Shapiro, 2002).

Behavior	Definition	Examples
On-Task Verbal	Any time the student is verbally engaged in the topic being taught.	Asking questions related to their work, talking to others about the work, answering questions when requested to do so.
On-Task Motor	Any time the student is actively attending to the assigned task.	Writing, raising a hand, and leaving their desk for a reason applicable to the assigned task.
On-Task Passive	Any time the student is passively attending to the assigned task.	Listening to the teacher, looking at their work, listening to a peer talk about the assigned task.
Off-Task Verbal	Any audible verbalizations that are not permitted or not related to the assigned task.	Talking to others about unrelated topics, making unauthorized comments, or noises.
Off-Task Motor	Any instance of motor activity that is not directly associated with the assigned academic task.	Reading or writing inappropriate or unassigned material, leaving the desk without receiving permission, physically touching other students.
Off-Task Passive	Any time a student is passively not attending to assigned academic task.	Gazing off, placing his head on the desk, looking at other students when not part of a given task.

Figure 2. Definitions and examples of on- and off-task behaviors.

Momentary time sampling gives an accurate estimate of percentage of time spent on and off task when brief intervals of less than 30 seconds are used (Saudargas & Zanolli, 1990). During pilot testing of the instrument the observers tested both 5-second and 10-second intervals. Ten second intervals were selected because it gave the observers enough time after recording an observation to visually locate the next participant. Each observer wore a wireless headset that transmitted a beep every ten seconds. At the moment the beep occurred the behavior of the participant was recorded, then the observer would visually locate the next participant on the list and wait for the next beep. Once all nine participants were recorded the observers would restart from the beginning of the list and continue recording the behaviors of participants until the 15 minutes were up. This resulted in approximately 10 observations per participant pre-lesson and 10 observations per participant post-lesson.

Data Analysis

On-task data was analyzed with SPSS 20.0. Mean on-task behavior was calculated as a percentage of time on-task for each participant at the beginning and end of each active and non-active lesson. Mean on-task behavior was then calculated for the entire class at all four time points (pre- and post-active lesson period, and pre- and post-non-active lesson period). Group series means were used to replace missing data from absentee participants (Tabachnick & Fidell, 2013). All data was checked for normality and significance was set at $p < 0.05$. A two-way, [time (beginning of lesson vs end of lesson) x period (active lesson vs. non-active lesson)] repeated measures ANOVA was conducted to determine if the pre-lesson and post-lesson on-task data were different depending on whether the data was from the non-active lesson period or active lesson period. Following a significant interaction paired t-tests were used to assess differences between the four factor levels.

Inter-rater Reliability

Prior to the study two observers were trained to conduct the on-task measurement. Observers reviewed and memorized the data collection protocol and the operational definitions for each observational category (on-task motor, on-task verbal, on-task passive, off-task motor, off-task verbal, and off-task passive). Observer training occurred in another elementary school with kindergarten and grade one students. The inter-rater reliability for the observers during training was found to be

Kappa = 0.615 (p < .0.001), 95% CI (0.788, 0.442). This indicates there was substantial agreement between the observers. During data collection for this study the second observer was present for 50% of the observation days, to ensure reliability of results and prevent observer bias. The inter-rater reliability for the actual study observations was found to be Kappa = 0.741 (p < .0.001), 95% CI (0.780, 0.702), again indicating substantial agreement.

Results

A two-way [time (pre lesson vs post lesson) x period (active lesson vs. non active lesson)] repeated measures ANOVA was conducted to determine if the classroom based physical activity intervention was successful in improving on-task behavior for participants. The analysis revealed a significant time x period interaction [$F_{(1, 8)}$ = 36.77, p < .001] (See Figure 3). The partial eta-squared was η^2 = 0.82.

In the NALP when the participants received no physical activity intervention there was a significant difference (p < .05) in on-task behavior scores from the beginning of the class to the end of the class (75% ± 11.9 to 69.6% ± 8.2). In contrast, during the ALP the students who received the MI intervention showed a significant difference (p < .001) in on-task behavior scores from the beginning of the lesson to the end of the lesson (70.6% ± 8.8 to 85.3% ± 10.2). Comparing the participant's on-task

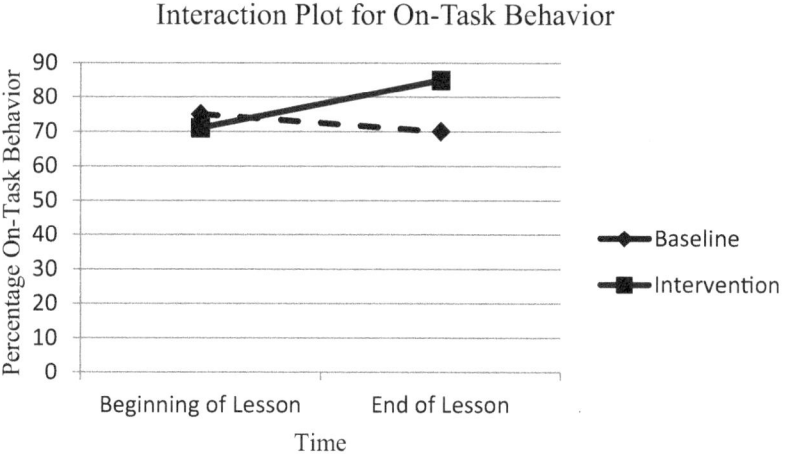

Figure 3. Interaction plot depicting statistically significant interaction [$F_{(1, 8)}$ =36.77, p < .001].

Table 1. Mean Percentages of On-Task Behavior

Percentage of on-task behavior	Non-active lessons		Active lessons	
	Beginning of lesson	End of lesson	Beginning of lesson	End of lesson
Mean	75	69.6	70.6	85.3
SD	11.9	8.2	8.8	10.2
Minimum	48.6	54.3	57.8	62.8
Maximum	87.1	77.1	85.4	95.4

scores at the end of NALP to their scores at the end of ALP, students were 15.7% more off-task at the end of class without the physical activity intervention than in the class with the intervention ($p < .05$). Although there was a difference in pre-observation scores in the NALP and ALP they were not statistically different ($p > .05$). Mean on-task behavior percentages are shown in Table 1.

Discussion

MI may enhance on-task behavior for Indigenous children in kindergarten and grade one. Our study results are consistent with previous research with non-Indigenous children that revealed on-task behavior improves with increased physical activity and, subsequently, decreases with the absence of physical activity. These findings further support the link between movement and self-regulation for young children. Emerging research demonstrates that physical activity has a positive effect on self-regulation and cognitive development in early childhood (Carlson et al., 2015). This stage of life is one of the most important periods for brain development, and physical activity can aid in facilitating optimal development (Carlson et al., 2015).

Our findings revealed that when the children did not receive a physical activity break in a 45-minute lesson their ability to stay on-task dropped significantly. Results from the present study also revealed that when students did get a short physical activity break in the middle of a lesson their ability to stay on-task increased from the beginning of the lesson to the end. These findings are consistent with the findings from classroom physical activity on-task research with preschool and older elementary school children (Becker et al., 2014; Harvey et al., 2018; Ma, Mare, & Gurd, 2014; Mahar et al., 2006; Palmer, Miller, & Robinson, 2013; Riley et al., 2015; Szabo-Reed et al., 2017).

This research may help support teachers in integrating physical activity in the school day. Teachers are generally supportive of the notion that physical activity is important for children, however they find it challenging to offer physical activity opportunities due to pressure to use their time for academic instruction (Ward et al., 2006). The MI used in this intervention mitigates this issue because it integrates academic content in the physical activity break. Based on the considerable increase in on-task behavior after the physical activity intervention one can argue that taking five minutes to get active has greater academic benefit than continuing with a sedentary lesson.

A strength of this study was the collaboration between the researcher, school leaders, and teachers in the Indigenous community. The PAR process produced relevant research done in a decolonizing way (Smith, 2013). Within physical activity and education research, there is a great need to develop interventions in collaboration with teachers and leaders in Indigenous communities so that the approaches, methods, and outcomes are meaningful to the communities (Mushquash & Bova, 2007; Oosman et al., 2016; Robinson, Borden, & Robinson, 2012). Collaborative process aligns with a culturally sustaining/revitalizing pedagogy approach that implements Indigenous education sovereignty, putting the power to make education decisions back in the hands of Indigenous communities and allowing them to reclaim and revitalize educational practices damaged by colonization (McCarty & Lee, 2014). Accountability through the development of respectful relationships, reciprocity, and responsibility are essential aspects of a culturally sustaining/revitalizing pedagogy approach (McCarty & Lee, 2014). Researchers interested in enhancing the educational experiences of Indigenous children through physical activity are encouraged to utilize a culturally sustaining/revitalizing pedagogy approach.

The participatory processes applied during this study speak to the primary goal of the Truth and Reconciliation Commission of Canada (TRC), which is to forge the important path to reconciliation for all people in Canada (Truth and Reconciliation Commission of Canada, 2015). After delegates spent six years listening to and learning from individuals, families, and communities affected by the residential school system the TRC released its final report in 2015. The Report's Calls to Action appeal to Indigenous and non-Indigenous communities and leaders to work together to eliminate the education gap between Indigenous and non-Indigenous Canadian children (The Truth and Reconciliation Commission of Canada, 2015). Addressing the current issues that affect Indigenous children's education is an important step in rectifying the injustices of the residential school system and colonization. This project sought to investigate one novel education method that can assist Indigenous children on their path to education success. To fully address education inequity, however, the nation must address unequal funding and expunge the larger issues of marginalization, colonization, and racism in education.

The parallels between Indigenous pedagogy and MI deserve special note. Indigenous pedagogy, based on the beliefs, values, history, and realities of Indigenous peoples, often focuses on experiential learning, service learning, learning through movement, and learning through enjoyment (Battiste, 2002; Preston et al., 2012). Students can embody Indigenous knowledge through games, songs, ceremonies, and symbols (Battiste, 2002). MI brings together academic content and movement, using songs, symbols, and games to teach children. Scholars and educators are currently developing and implementing pedagogical experiences for Indigenous children that incorporate physical games and outdoor learning experiences that require physical activity (Dubosarsky et al., 2011; Hansen, 2018; Miller, Doering, Roehrig, & Shimek, 2012). A strong momentum within the physical activity research community works to develop culturally responsive physical education, which embeds Indigenous worldviews, perspectives, and cultural values (Halas, McCrae, & Carpenter, 2013; Robinson et al., 2012). Future research should continue to explore the strong link between movement and Indigenous pedagogy. An emerging body of literature has grown over the past two decades showing that children who move more learn better (de Greeff et al., 2018). Indigenous knowledge keepers have known this reality and incorporated it in Indigenous pedagogy since time immemorial. The time has come to fully bring movement back into learning.

One limitation to this study is that the intervention was not adapted to include Indigenous themes, symbols, language, or traditional knowledge. Indigenizing the MI intervention would have required far more extensive community input from language keepers, Elders, and others richly endowed with Indigenous knowledge. Many assume that Indigenous teachers have extensive knowledge of Indigenous pedagogy and are informed on Indigenous language and culture, but the reality is that many Indigenous teachers feel just as unprepared as non-Indigenous teachers who are asked to incorporate Indigenous knowledge into their practice (St. Denis, Bouvier, & Battiste, 1998). This fact, coupled with the scientific benefit of replicating the *Energizers* activities as they were used in studies that improved on-task behavior (Mahar et al., 2006), obliged the researcher to use a physical activity intervention that was developed from a Euro-Western perspective.

Future researchers who seek to develop physical activity interventions with Indigenous communities should take into consideration if Indigenous teachers in the community feel they have the competence and confidence to bring Indigenous pedagogy into their classrooms and aid in the development of a culturally responsive intervention (Kitchen, Cherubini, Trudeau, & Hodson, 2010). When Indigenous teachers possess cultural competence and confidence in the ways in which culture benefits students, they can play an important role in enhancing the educational experience of their Indigenous students (Castagno & Brayboy, 2008; Yazzie-Mintz, 2007). Indigenous teachers need to be encouraged to bring their Indigenous self to the classroom and have confidence in sharing Indigenous knowledge with their students, knowing that the knowledge is valuable and that they are supported in bringing it into the classroom (Yazzie-Mintz, 2007). When Indigenous teachers are not familiar with their own culture, they should be supported in re-learning their language, traditions, knowledge, and stories (Yazzie-Mintz, 2007). This method can be embedded within future educational intervention designs, as integrating Indigenous knowledge into educational interventions is impractical without teachers shaping and implementing that knowledge.

Lastly, interventions with early Indigenous learners should include curriculum which represents community-specific worldviews and promotes valued behaviors. For early learners curriculum could include Indigenous language and music, traditional stories that teach important lessons, Indigenous history, and Indigenous science. For example, MI activities that involve animal sounds and movements could substitute animals important to the local community for farm animals. An active math exercise could use numbers from the students' Indigenous language instead of English. The inclusion of meaningful and relevant Indigenous curriculum can affirm Indigenous students' cultural identities (Halas et al., 2013).

Conclusion

Findings from this study indicated that MI may assist young Indigenous learners in staying on-task, an important learning behavior associated with self-regulation. The benefits of MI are many; it can be easier to implement than other types of physical activity because it is done in the classroom and does not require equipment, gym scheduling, or special clothes. MI also aligns with the values and ways of learning represented in Indigenous pedagogy. MI activities that promote physical activity are easily accessible through the Internet and can be easily adapted to fit most curriculums and classroom needs, including adapting the activities to include Indigenous pedagogy. Because of the academic benefits of physical activity, teachers should be encouraged and supported by school administrators and leaders to incorporate more physical activity in the day for children in their first years of school.

Serene Kerpan is an assistant professor in the Faculty of Health Sciences at University of Ontario Institute of Technology. Through community-engaged scholarship she cultivates strong relationships with Indigenous schools and communities to investigate the effect of physical activity on the well-being of Indigenous children and youth.

M. Louise Humbert is a professor in the College of Kinesiology at the University of Saskatchewan. She is a past president of Physical and Health Education Canada.

Carol D. Rodgers is a associate professor in the College of Kinesiology at the University of Saskatchewan.

Alexandra L. Stoddart is an assistant professor in the Health, Outdoor, and Physical Education (HOPE) subject area in the Faculty of Education at the University of Regina.

REFERENCES

Allen, J., Mohatt, G. V., Markstrom, C. A., Byers, L., & Novins, D. K. (2012). "Oh no, we are just getting to know you": The relationship in research with children and youth in indigenous communities. *Child Development Perspectives, 6*(1), 55–60.

Battiste, M. (1998). Enabling the autumn seed: Toward a decolonized approach to Aboriginal knowledge, language, and education. *Canadian Journal of Native Education, 22*(1), 16.

Battiste, M. (2002). *Indigenous knowledge and pedagogy in First Nations education: A literature review with recommendations.* Ottawa, ON: Apamuwek Institute.

Baum, F., MacDougall, C., & Smith, D. (2006). Participatory action research. *Journal of Epidemiology and Community Health, 60,* 854–857. doi:10.1136/jech.2004.028662.

Becker, D. R., McClelland, M. M., Loprinzi, P., & Trost, S. G. (2014). Physical activity, self-regulation, and early academic achievement in preschool children. *Early Education and Development, 25*(1), 56–70. doi:10.1080/10409289.2013.780505.

Blair, C. (2002). School readiness: Integrating cognition and emotion in a neurobiological conceptualization of children's functioning at school entry. *American Psychologist, 57*(2), 111–127.

Blair, C., & Razza, R. P. (2007). Relating effortful control, executive function, and false belief understanding to emerging math and literacy ability in kindergarten. *Child Development, 78*(2), 647–663.

Brayboy, B. M. J., & Maaka, M. J. (2015). K–12 achievement for Indigenous students. *Journal of American Indian Education, 54*(1), 63–98.

Cajete, G. A. (2005). American Indian epistemologies. *New Directions for Student Services, 109,* 69–78.

Canadian Council on Learning. (2009). *The state of Aboriginal learning in Canada: A holistic approach to measuring success.* Retrieved from https://www.afn.ca/uploads/files/education2/state_of_aboriginal_learning_in_canada-final_report,_ccl,_2009.pdf.

Canadian Institutes of Health Research, Natural Sciences and Engineering Research Council of Canada, and the Social Sciences and Humanities Research Council of Canada. (2014). *Tri-Council policy statement: Ethical conduct for research involving humans.* Ottawa, ON: Public Works and Government Services Canada.

Carlson, J. A, Engelberg, J. K., Cain, K. L., Conway, T. L., Mignano, A. M., Bonilla, E. A., . . . & Sallis, J. F. (2015). Implementing classroom physical activity breaks: Associations with student physical activity and classroom behavior. *Preventive Medicine, 81,* 67–72. doi:10.1016/j.ypmed.2015.08.006.

Carson, V., Hunter, S., Kuzik, N., Wiebe, S. A., Spence, J. C., Friedman, A., . . . & Hinkley, T. (2016). Systematic review of physical activity and cognitive development in early childhood. *Journal of Science and Medicine in Sport, 19*(7), 573–578.

Castagno, A. E., & Brayboy, B. M. J. (2008). Culturally responsive schooling for Indigenous youth: A review of the literature. *Review of Educational Research, 78*(4), 941–993.

Castellano, M. B. (2004). Ethics of Aboriginal research. *Journal of Aboriginal Health,* January, 98.

Castelli, D. M., Centeio, E. E., Hwang, J., Barcelona, J. M., Glowacki, E. M., Calvert, H. G., & Nicksic, H. M. (2014). The history of physical activity and academic performance research: informing the future. *Monographs of the Society for Research in Child Development, 79*(4), 119–48. doi:10.1111/mono .12133.

Constitution Act of Canada. (1982). Retrieved from http://laws-lois.justice.gc.ca/eng/const.

de Greeff, J. W., Bosker, R. J., Oosterlaan, J., Visscher, C., & Hartman, E. (2018). Effects of physical activity on executive functions, attention and academic performance in preadolescent children: a meta-analysis. *Journal of Science and Medicine in Sport, 21* (5), 501–507.

Dubosarsky, M., Murphy, B., Roehrig, G., Frost, L. C., Jones, J., Carlson, S. P., & Bement, J. (2011). Incorporating cultural themes to promote preschoolers' critical thinking in American Indian head start classrooms. *Young Children, 66*(5), 20–29.

Faircloth, S. C. (2015). The early childhood education of American Indian and Alaska Native children: State of the research. *Journal of American Indian Education, 54*(1), 99–126.

Faul, F., Erdfelder, E., Buchner, A., & Lang, A. G. (2009). Statistical power analyses using G*Power 3.1: tests for correlation and regression analyses. *Behavior Research Methods, 41*(4), 1149–60.

First Peoples Worldwide (2016). *Who are Indigenous peoples.* Retrieved from http://www.firstpeoples.org/who-are-indigenous-peoples.

Grieco, L. A., Jowers, E. M., & Bartholomew, J. B. (2009). Physically active academic lessons and time on task: the moderating effect of body mass index. *Medicine and Science in Sports and Exercise, 41*(10), 1921–6. doi:10.1249/MSS.0b013e3181a61495.

Guo, Y., Logan, H. L., Glueck, D. H., & Muller, K. E. (2013). Selecting a sample size for studies with repeated measures. *BMC Medical Research Methodology, 13*(1), 100.

Halas, J., McCrae, H., & Carpenter, A. (2013). The quality and cultural relevance of physical education for Aboriginal youth: Challenges and opportunities. In J. Forsythe & A. R. Giles (Eds.). *Aboriginal peoples and sport in Canada: Historical foundations and contemporary issues* (pp. 182–205). Vancouver, BC: University of British Columbia Press.

Hansen, J. (2018). Cree elders' perspectives on land-based education: A case study. *Brock Education: A Journal of Educational Research and Practice, 28*(1), 74–91.

Harvey, S. P., Lambourne, K., Greene, J. L., Gibson, C. A., Lee, J., & Donnelly, J. E. (2018). The effects of physical activity on learning behaviors in elementary school children: A randomized controlled trial. *Contemporary School Psychology, 22*(3), 303–312.

Henrich, J., Heine, S. J., & Norenzayan, A. (2010). The weirdest people in the world? *Behavioral and Brain Sciences, 33*(2–3), 61–83.

Hintze, J. M., Volpe, R. J., & Shapiro, E. S. (2002). Best practices in the systematic direct observation of student behavior. *School Psychology Review, 34*(4), 993–1006.

Israel, B., Eng, E., Schulz, A., & Parker, E. (2005). Introduction to Methods for Community-Based Participatory Methods for Health: Methods. In B. Israel, E. Eng, A. Schulz & E. Parker (Eds.). *Methods in Community-Based Participatory Research for Health* (pp. 1–3). San Francisco, CA: Jossey-Bass.

Kerpan, S., Humbert, M. L., & Abonyi, S. (2019). Perceptions of Canadian Indigenous teachers and students on movement integration in the classroom. *The Australian Journal of Indigenous Education, 1-10.*

Kirk, S. M., Vizcarra, C. R., Looney, E. C., & Kirk, E. P. (2014). Using physical activity to teach academic content: A study of the effects on literacy in Head Start preschoolers. *Early Childhood Education Journal, 42,* 181–189. doi:10.1007/s10643-013-0596-3

Kitchen, J., Cherubini, L., Trudeau, L., & Hodson, J. (2010). Weeding out or developing capacity? Challenges for Aboriginal teacher education. *Alberta Journal of Educational Research, 56*(2), 104–123.

LeCuyer, E. A., & Zhang, Y. (2015). An integrative review of ethnic and cultural variation in socialization and children's self-regulation. *Journal of Advanced Nursing, 71*(4), 735–750.

Ma, J. K., Mare, L. L., & Gurd, B. J. (2014). Classroom-based high-intensity interval activity improves off-task behaviour in primary school students. *Applied Physiology, Nutrition, and Metabolism, 39*(12), 1332–1337.

Mahar, M., Kenny, R., Shields, A., Scales, D., & Collins, G. (2010). *Energizers: Classroom-based physical activities.* Retrieved from https://www.ecu.edu/cs-hhp/exss/upload/Energizers_for_Grades_3_5.pdf.

Mahar, M. T. (2011). Impact of short bouts of physical activity on attention-to-task in elementary school children. *Preventive Medicine, 52 (Suppl. 1),* S60–4.

Mahar, M. T., Murphy, S. K., Rowe, D. A, Golden, J., Shields, A. T., & Raedeke, T. D. (2006). Effects of a classroom-based program on physical activity and on-task behavior. *Medicine and Science in Sports and Exercise, 38*(12), 2086–94. doi:10.1249/01.mss.0000235359.16685.a3

Marks, A. K., & Coll, C. G. (2007). Psychological and demographic correlates of early academic skill development among American Indian and Alaska Native youth: A growth modeling study. *Developmental Psychology, 43*(3), 663.

McCarty, T. L., & Lee, T. S. (2014). Critical culturally sustaining/revitalizing pedagogy and Indigenous education sovereignty. *Harvard Educational Review, 84*(1), 101–124.

McClelland, M. M., & Cameron, C. E. (2011). Self-regulation and academic achievement in elementary school children. *New Directions for Child and Adolescent Development, 133,* 29–44. doi:10.1002/cd

McHugh, T. L. F., Kingsley, B. C., & Coppola, A. M. (2013). Enhancing the relevance of physical activity research by engaging Aboriginal peoples in the research process. *Pimatisiwin, 11*(2), 293–305.

Miller, B. G., Doering, A., Roehrig, G., & Shimek, R. (2012). Fostering Indigenous STEM education: Mobilizing the Adventure Learning Framework through snow snakes. *Journal of American Indian Education, 51*(2), 67.

Mushquash, C. J., & Bova, D. L. (2007). Cross-cultural assessment and measurement issues. *Journal on Developmental Disabilities, 13*(1), 53–65.

Niles, M., Byers, L., & Krueger, E. (2007). Best practice and evidence-based research in Indigenous early childhood intervention programs. *Canadian Journal of Native Education, 30*(1), 108.

Oosman, S., Smylie, J., Humbert, L., & Henry, C. (2016). Métis community perspectives inform a school-based health promotion intervention using participatory action. *Engaged Scholar Journal, 1*(2), 58–76.

Palmer, K. K., Miller, M. W., & Robinson, L. E. (2013). Acute exercise enhances preschoolers' ability to sustain attention. *Journal of Sport and Exercise Psychology, 35,* 433–437.

Preston, J. P., Cottrell, M., Pelletier, T. R., & Pearce, J. V. (2012). Aboriginal early childhood education in Canada: Issues of context. *Journal of Early Childhood Research, 10*(1), 3–18.

Riley, N., Lubans, D. R., Morgan, P. J., & Young, M. (2015). Outcomes and process evaluation of a programme integrating physical activity into the primary school mathematics curriculum: The EASY Minds pilot randomised controlled trial. *Journal of Science and Medicine in Sport, 18*(6), 656–661.

Rimm-Kaufman, S. E., Curby, T. W., Grimm, K. J., Nathanson, L., & Brock, L. L. (2009). The contribution of children's self-regulation and classroom quality to children's adaptive behaviors in the kindergarten classroom. *Developmental Psychology, 45*(4), 958.

Rimm-Kaufman, S. E., Pianta, R. C., & Cox, M. J. (2000). Teachers' judgments of problems in the transition to kindergarten. *Early Childhood Research Quarterly, 15*(2), 147–166. doi:10.1016/S0885-2006(00)00049-1

Robinson, D. B., Borden, L. L., & Robinson, I. M. (2012). Charting a course for culturally responsive physical education. *Alberta Journal of Educational Research, 58*(4), 526–546.

Romero-Little, M. E. (2010). How should young Indigenous children be prepared for learning? A vision of early childhood education for Indigenous children. *Journal of American Indian Education, 49*(1/2), 7–27.

Sarche, M. C., & Whitesell, N. R. (2012). Child development research in North American native communities—Looking back and moving forward. *Child Development Perspectives, 6*(1), 42–48.

Saudargas, R., & Zanolli, K. (1990). Momentary time sampling as an estimate of percentage time-A field validation. *Journal of Applied Behavior Analysis, 23*(4), 533–537.

Schmidt, M., Egger, F., Benzing, V., Jäger, K., Conzelmann, A., Roebers, C. M., & Pesce, C. (2017). Disentangling the relationship between children's motor ability, executive function and academic achievement. *PloS One, 12*(8), e0182845.

Shapiro, E. S. (2011). *Academic skills problems: Direct assessment and intervention.* (2nd ed.). New York, NY: Guilford Press.

Smith, L. T. (2013). *Decolonizing methodologies: Research and Indigenous peoples.* London, UK: Zed Books.

Smylie, J., & Anderson, M. (2006). Understanding the health of Indigenous peoples in Canada: key methodological and conceptual challenges. *Canadian Medical Association Journal, 175*(6), 602–602.

Spicer, P., LaFramboise, T., Markstrom, C., Niles, M., West, A., Fehringer, K., . . . & Sarche, M. (2012). Toward an applied developmental science for Native children, families, and communities. *Child Development Perspectives, 6*(1), 49–54.

St. Denis, V., Bouvier, R., & Battiste, M. (1998) *Okiskinahamakewak-Aboriginal teachers in Saskatchewan public schools: Responding to the flux.* Regina, SK: Saskatchewan Education Research Networking Project.

Szabo-Reed, A. N., Willis, E. A., Lee, J., Hillman, C. H., Washburn, R. A., & Donnelly, J. E. (2017). Impact of three years of classroom physical activity bouts on time-on-task behavior. *Medicine and Science in Sports and Exercise, 49*(11), 2343–2350.

Tabachnick, B., & Fidell, L. (2013). *Using multivariate statistics* (6th ed.) Boston, MA: Pearson.

Truth and Reconciliation Commission of Canada. (2015). *Honouring the truth, reconciling for the future.* Retrieved from http://nctr.ca/assets/reports/Final%20 Reports/Executive_Summary_English_Web.pdf.

Wagner, B., Fitzpatrick, J., Symons, M., Jirikowic, T., Cross, D., & Latimer, J. (2017). The development of a culturally appropriate school-based intervention for Australian Aboriginal children living in remote communities: A formative evaluation of the Alert Program® intervention. *Australian Occupational Therapy Journal, 64*(3), 243–252.

Waldram, J. B., Herring, A., & Young, T. K. (2006). *Aboriginal health in Canada: historical, cultural, and epidemiological perspectives.* Toronto, ON: University of Toronto Press.

Ward, D. S., Saunders, R., Felton, G. M., Williams, E., Epping, J. N., & Pate, R. R. (2006). Implementation of a school environment intervention to increase physical activity in high school girls. *Health Education Research, 21*(6), 896–910.

Webster, C. A., Russ, L., Vazou, S., Goh, T., & Erwin, H. (2015). Integrating movement in academic classrooms: Understanding, applying, and advancing the knowledge base. *Obesity Reviews, 16,* 691–701.

White, J. P., & Peters, J. (2013). Editors' Commentary: The challenges in improving Indigenous educational attainment. *The International Indigenous Policy Journal, 4*(4). doi 10.18584/iipj.2013.4.4.6

Wilson, C. (2001). Review of the book *Decolonizing methodologies: Research and Indigenous peoples,* by L. T. Smith. *Social Policy Journal of New Zealand, 17,* 214–218.

Yazzie-Mintz, T. (2007). From a place deep inside: Culturally appropriate curriculum as the embodiment of Navajo-ness in classroom pedagogy. *Journal of American Indian Education, 46*(3), 72–93.

Reports From the Field

Indigenous Research Perspectives in the State of New Mexico: Implications for Working With Schools and Communities

ROBIN ZAPE-TAH-HOL-AH MINTHORN,
LORENDA BELONE, GLENABAH MARTINEZ,
AND CHRISTINE SIMS

This article introduces the Indigenous research perspectives of four Native faculty who have engaged their colleagues in the College of Education (COE) at the University of New Mexico (UNM) toward a deeper understanding of the relationship among research, sovereignty, and honoring the integrity of tribal nations. The article is a theoretical/conceptual presentation of the multiple factors and conditions that affect Indigenous research and the implications for working with schools and communities. Specifically, the authors introduce a framework to guide research conducted in Indigenous nations in New Mexico. Major elements of the framework include (a) a historical overview of sovereignty in the context of the State of New Mexico, (b) an analysis of tribal powers within the framework of sovereignty, and (c) an overview of research guidelines. The sources for this paper emerge from individual research protocols and frameworks utilized by the four Indigenous faculty at UNM and the heartwork done with Native nations in New Mexico.

COMMUNITY ENGAGEMENT WITH NATIVE NATIONS in New Mexico is at the core of teaching, service, and scholarship for faculty in the Institute for American Indian Education (IAIE) at the University of New Mexico (UNM). Cultivating authentic relationships with Native nations is critical for sustaining a culture of responsiveness and reciprocity. There are 24 Native nations in New Mexico that include the Navajo Nation, the 20 Pueblo Nations, and three Apache Nations. In this article, we present a historical overview of government-to-government relations between the Native nations and state government, an analysis of tribal powers, an overview of research guidelines that frame our work at UNM, and a discussion of the implications for Indigenous education in the state of New Mexico. This is particularly urgent given the recent ruling of *Yazzie/Martinez v. State of New Mexico*, which challenged the New Mexico Public Education Department and state legislature for failure to provide "low income, Native American, English language learner (ELL), and students with disabilities [with] programs and services for them to learn and thrive" (New Mexico Center on Law and Poverty, 2018, para. 2).

Indigenous peoples across the hemisphere and in the region now known as New Mexico have always exercised sovereignty and self-determination since time immemorial. In the case of the Pueblo Nations of New Mexico, the nation-to-nation relationship predated the formation of the United States in the 18th century with the Spanish *entrada* in the 16th century. Forbes (1994) estimates that at the time of the entrada there were between 70 and 100 distinct Pueblo Nations in the Southwest, and by the late 17th century the number was reduced to 19.

Each Pueblo Nation lived relatively independent of one another from the northernmost Pueblo Nation of Taos, south to Isleta, and west to Zuni. Jemez scholar Joe Sando (1998) describes the semi-autonomous relationship of the Pueblo Nations.

> The nineteen pueblos share a common traditional native religion, although rituals and observances may vary; a similar lifestyle and philosophy; and a common economy based on the same geographical region occupied by them for thousands of years. But the pueblos have an independence similar to that of nations; although they are in close proximity to one another, and subject to the same natural forces, each maintains a unique identity. Thus the pueblos have common elements, but are distinctive entities in their own right. (p. 8)

The Pueblo Nations are not the only Indigenous peoples in this region, however. The Diné, Jicarilla Apache, and Mescalero Apache Nations have also existed as sovereign nations since time immemorial.

Diné Bikéyah, or Navajoland, extends into the current states of Utah, Arizona, and New Mexico. Diné scholar Jennifer Denetdale (2006) describes Navajo political autonomy:

> Prior to Euro-American invasion, the Diné, who by all accounts were an autonomous people, who became wealthy when sheep and horses were integrated into their society, practiced their own system of government,

albeit not one that was seen as rational or acceptable to Euro-Americans. The fundamental Navajo political entity, called a "natural community," was composed of local bands that consisted of ten to forty families. In the largest assembly, called a naachid, which was a regional gathering, twenty-four headmen, twelve of whom were peace leaders and twelve of whom were war leaders, met to address internal matters, intertribal affairs, hunting, and food gathering. (p. 11)

The sovereign status of the Diné Nation is currently acknowledged by the Navajo Nation with an 1868 treaty negotiated with the U.S. government when they returned from Bosque Redondo (Hwéeldi, also known as Fort Sumner, New Mexico) to their homeland. Navajo Sovereignty Day takes place on the fourth Monday in April each year. However, it is important to note that the Diné exercised sovereignty prior to 1868. In a 2012 speech to the Navajo Nation on Sovereignty Day, President Ben Shelly stated, "On this day, we must remember our leaders who fought to ensure our sovereignty as the Navajo Nation. We have always been a sovereign nation, and on this day we must think about how we are going to ensure our nation's sovereign strength in the future" (Indian Country Today Media Network, 2012, para. 2).

The historical narratives of the Jicarilla Apache Nation and the Mescalero Apache Nation also provide a historical record of sovereign status. Drawing on the historical record established by Jicarilla scholar Veronica Tiller, Nordhaus, Hall, and Rudio (2003) summarize their origin history.

As the Jicarillas would tell it, all life on earth originated from the Jemez Mountains. . . . Marked by the boundaries of four sacred rivers: the Arkansas, Canadian, Rio Grande, and Pecos, the traditional territory of the Jicarilla Apache stretched over 50 million acres. The Jicarillas deemed this homeland "near the center of the earth." (p. 249)

In the mid-nineteenth century, the Jicarilla were forced out of their homeland in northern New Mexico through settler colonialism. Forced displacement resulted in their relocation to live with the Mescalero Apache Nation in south-central New Mexico. Through a federal Executive Order on February 11, 1887, the Jicarilla Nation was allotted a small tract of land 16 miles wide and 30 miles long near current-day Dulce, New Mexico. This land was not part of their traditional homelands. In 1907 their landholdings were increased. Throughout this period, the Jicarilla maintained their cultural traditions and traditional governance.

According to Tiller (1983), "[T]here was no formal political organization among the Jicarilla, but there was a hierarchy of leading religious leaders, warriors, and politicians who dealt with other tribes and the Spaniards and Americans" (p. 443).

Prior to contact with Spaniards, the Mescalero Apache people moved freely throughout the Southwest. The Mescalero Apache reservation was established by Executive Order on May 29, 1873, by President Ulysses S. Grant. The reservation became the central place for relocating three bands of Apaches—Chiricahua, Lipan, and Mescalero. The Mescalero Apache homelands included the current reservation and greater Southwest regions of Texas, Arizona, and Mexico. The Lipan Apache, whose original homelands spanned from what is now Texas to Mexico, were relocated to Mescalero in the early 1900s. A few hundred Chiricahua Apaches who were imprisoned at Fort Sill, Oklahoma, were moved to Mescalero around 1913. The Chiricahua Apache homelands spanned throughout Arizona and Mexico. While the creation of the Mescalero Apache reservation is fairly recent, the histories of the three bands of Apaches span hundreds of years. When the Tribe reorganized in 1936, the three bands became Mescalero Apache Tribal members, but families today still connect to their ancestral bands (http://mescaleroapachetribe.com/our-culture). Similar to the 19 Pueblo Nations, the Diné Nation, and the Jicarilla Apache Nation, the Mescalero people sustained a strong cultural and political life as a sovereign entity prior to 1873. Leadership and governance, according to Opler (1983), occurred through a nant'á (he who commands, leads, directs, and/or advises), who "was sensitive to the views of other family heads and sought consensus rather than the acceptance of his own personal views" (p. 429).

The 24 Indigenous nations described here continue to exercise sovereignty. It should be noted that in November 2011 a reservation was established for the Fort Sill Apache Nation in New Mexico. The website of the New Mexico Indian Affairs Department (2017) describes the state's 23 sovereign nations:

> Each Tribe is a sovereign nation with its own government, life-ways, traditions, and culture; and each tribe has a unique relationship with the federal and state governments. The twenty-three tribes in New Mexico are actively engaged to preserve their indigenous languages, religion, culture, the environment and in promoting quality education and health care for all members, especially their youth and elders. Economic development as a means to achieve these goals is important to Tribal leadership as is homeland security and housing for their communities. (para. 1 & 2)

Recognizing sovereignty exercised by the 24 Native nations of New Mexico is critical to our work as Indigenous faculty at a Research I university. Our responsibility includes the education of non-Native faculty in understanding the dialectical relationship among research, sovereignty, and honoring the integrity of tribal nations.

In understanding this complex existence and lived reality as Indigenous scholars at the UNM College of Education (COE), it is our responsibility to educate and advocate for the accountability, understanding, and respect that should be afforded to each tribal community with whom our colleagues, programs, and departments work. There should always be, as well, a consideration of how such work will impact the survival of language and culture among tribal communities in New Mexico. It is through this understanding, therefore, that we begin to build a baseline of critical consciousness in connecting the concepts of sovereignty to political autonomy of tribal nations and Indigenous peoples in New Mexico.

Analysis of Tribal Powers Within the Framework of Sovereignty

Within New Mexico, under the administration of former governor Bill Richardson (2003–2011), an official state policy of tribal consultation was established, requiring each major state department and agency to consult with New Mexico tribes and nations any time state government policies, laws or services affect the state's 24 tribes. An evolution of this policy is demonstrated through the government-to-government relations. For example, the state's Office of Indian Education facilitates biannual government-to-government meetings to address critical issues related to education. At the core of sovereignty are the foundations that have enabled tribal nations and societies to thrive as viable cultures and linguistic communities for centuries. These foundations are centered upon core values that have operated as key elements in maintaining cultural integrity in the face of historic colonization by various foreign regimes. The core values of respect, service, reciprocity, balance, and maintaining relationships that bind a people together are examples of lived principles at work in these communities. They also reflect the critical nature and role that tribal leadership has played in exercising agency on behalf of their people.

This recent state policy recognized that tribal nations are in the position of accepting or rejecting state policies and services that they determine to be either beneficial or contrary to the needs or interests of their communities. By extension, state policies on consultation must therefore also be recognized by the state's institutions of higher education and their agents. Unfortunately, this is rarely reflected in the research paradigms and processes employed by university faculty and the students they mentor when such research involves Native people and/or their communities.

Our intent as Native faculty within the COE during the recent process of reimagining the preparation of preservice teachers was to educate our colleagues about the unique parameters surrounding health and education research with tribal communities as we worked alongside them in this college-wide initiative. This has been a unique challenge, as academic paradigms for research influence much of the thinking behind how and what this looks like from a purely institutional perspective.

Overview of Research Guidelines

"History is a narration about past events that tells us about what was important when the event or era occurred, but also about what we think about the event today" (Roberts, 2007, as cited in Oetzel, 2009, p. 339). For many Native communities, their past and their narratives or stories about their history were shared orally from one generation to the next because most Native languages had no written traditions. So, in a sense, although it is the actual event(s) that define the past, it is the stories and narratives that make up history and our history reflects what we want to remember and how we see ourselves and others (Darnton, 2003; Loewen, 1999; Roberts, 2007; Oetzel, 2009). Oetzel (2009) describes three reasons that history is important: (a) it is part of collective memory and cultural identity; (b) past traumatic events are passed down through generations (historical trauma); and (c) history has significant consequences for intercultural relations today. The telling of history is an important aspect of many cultures because it contextualizes important events from the past, now, and into the future (Belone, 2010); however, history has been told from the colonizers' perspectives but that is changing and there are now Native scholars who are rewriting their own tribal histories resulting in "transformative scholarship" (Lee, 2010, p. 44).

At UNM the COE recognizes the critical role that health has in the education of Indigenous people. Therefore, we will highlight health research situated in an Indigenous context.

Historically, research has been conducted on Native communities with no benefit to individual members or to the tribe as a whole and it has frequently inflicted long-lasting harm resulting in historical trauma (Brave Heart, 2003; Whitbeck, Adams, Hoyt, & Chen, 2004). For that reason, the history of research on tribal communities can quickly conjure many negative narratives. According to Christopher, Watts, McCormick, and Young (2008), many Native communities have been "analyzed, stereotyped, and exploited by outside groups" (p. 1398) as research subjects. These negative experiences have created memories of historical mistreatment (Baldwin, Johnson, & Benally, 2009; Burhans-stipanov, Christopher, & Schumacher, 2005; Davis & Reid, 1999; Wallerstein & Duran, 2010). The many historical abuses imposed on Native communities in the name of health research is remembered histories (narratives) that have lingering effects (Belone, 2010), resulting in a mistrust of research by tribe communities (Smith, 2012).

Unfortunately, the historical mistrust of research and researchers by Native communities has hampered the work of Native researchers today who are genuinely interested in conducting health disparities research (Christopher et al., 2008). It is not uncommon for Native people to feel as if they have been "researched to death" with no benefit(s) except for stigmatizing findings that, for the most part, benefit only the investigator(s) and the academic institution(s) (Burhansstipanov et al., 2005; Davis & Reid, 1999; Walters & Simoni, 2009). Interestingly, this was the exact sentiment that was voiced at a Tribal Council meeting about a newly funded National Institutes of Health (NIH) health research study presented by one of the authors of this article. The council was quick to inform the Native faculty about their experience with past researchers and their disinterest in research. The Native faculty informed the council that she would not utilize the traditional approach to research but instead a community-based participatory approach which interested the Tribal Council, who ultimately passed a resolution agreeing to a research partnership.

Fortunately, the health literature is rich with recommendations on building research partnerships with Native communities especially in areas related to the investigation of health disparities (Baldwin et al., 2009; Belone et al., 2012; Belone et al., 2016; Burhansstipanov et al., 2005; LaVeaux & Christopher, 2009; Wallerstein & Duran, 2006). Recommendations often include the use of decolonizing strategies (Fisher & Ball, 2005; LaVeaux & Christopher, 2009; Smith, 2012; Wallerstein & Duran, 2006; Walters & Simoni, 2009), with a participatory approach involving the community which has been defined by the W. K. Kellogg Foundation's 2001 Community Health Scholars Program as community—based participatory research (CBPR)—"a collaborative approach to research that equitably involves all partners in the research process and recognizes the unique strengths that each bring" (Minkler & Wallerstein, 2008, p. 6, as cited in Belone, 2010). Thus, positive research partnerships between Native communities and universities are in fact possible and can produce mutual benefits, resulting in a growing capacity by these communities to be active partners in the research process.

Over the past decade, Native communities have demanded that health studies provide a benefit to the community. Written guidelines and/or tribal institutional review boards have also been established with the required recognition of tribal sovereignty, data ownership, and approval of all publication(s) (Becenti-Pigman, White, Bowman, Palmanteer-Holder, & Duran, 2008; Belone et al., 2016; NCAI Policy Research Center and MSU Center for Native Health Partnerships, 2012; Straits et al., 2012). In the academy there has also been an active movement primarily by Native scholars in the development of research policies regarding Native communities (e.g., an American Indian/Alaskan Native Research Policy and Procedure for the University of New Mexico Health Sciences Center under review), and guidelines such as the Guiding Principles for Engaging in Research with Native American Communities (Straits et al., 2012), outlining recommendations on engaging Native communities in the research process that move away from the traditional paradigm of being "researched on" to a more equal research partnership that reflects "research with," a welcome positive change for the future.

In the last decade and a half, a few national initiatives have focused on Native health with the aims of reducing American Indian/Alaska Native health disparities while overcoming the "distrust of research" and developing "a pipeline of Native researchers" (Belone, Griffith, & Baquero, 2018). In 2000, NIH, in partnership with the Indian Health Service, created the Native American Research Centers for Health (NARCH). This unique program funded numerous successful research projects in which the funds were disturbed to tribes or a tribally based organization, who then collaborated with an academic partner. NARCH is currently in its tenth cycle of funding. A more recent NIH initiative, the Intervention Research to Improve Native American Health (IRINAH), which involves funding opportunities to develop a "community of scientists to expand the knowledge base regarding intervention science with Indigenous populations" (Gittelsohn et al., 2018, p. 3) through the incorporation of Indigenous community perspectives while utilizing Indigenous research methods by Indigenous researchers, this actively engaged network of investigators is focused on reducing health disparities in tribal communities across the country (Crump, Etz, Arroyo, Hemberger, & Srinivasan, 2017; Dickerson et al., 2018; Gittelsohn et al., 2018).

Implications and Applications

In this section we highlight the direct implications of having Indigenous faculty who have advocated for and acknowledge the important role in building relationships with tribal nations in the State of New Mexico and across the United States. This also requires advocacy in incorporating Indigenous education efforts through the development of Indigenous-focused research conferences, graduate courses, programs, and MOUs. This section highlights how research and community engagement are inextricably linked. The focus is on community and less on individual pursuits of recognition within the Western paradigm of research and scholarship.

Indigenous Education Research Conference

With the collaboration of the authors and other Indigenous faculty in UNM's COE, the First Annual Indigenous Education Research Conference (IERC) emerged in 2016. The conference's inaugural theme was "Education, Power, and Indigenous Communities." The idea for the conference originated from a course developed by Dr. Glenabah Martinez in the mid-1990s for UNM's Native American Studies curriculum. Similar to the course, the conference focused on the social, cultural, political, geopolitical, and economic contexts in which Indigenous peoples engage in education. The uniqueness of IERC is that it is a two-day conference that intentionally included youth and community and incorporated visits to Indigenous community-based sites in Albuquerque and local tribal communities. Based on the success of the first IERC and at the request of the participating Indigenous communities, a second IERC was held in 2017 with a conference theme of "Indigenous Education and Activism: What Is Your Contribution?" This second conference was equally successful. The purpose of the IERC conference is to honor the cultural integrity and sovereignty in relation to Indigenous education.

Establishing a Graduate Research Methods Course Focused on Indigenous Research Paradigms

As a result of understanding the importance of cultural sovereignty and political autonomy, the need to address Indigenous research paradigms and an overview of the research guidelines discussed above also emerged in a graduate research methods course. Such a course would provide an opportunity for all graduate students across COE departments and programs to expand their knowledge about these issues. As a collaborative effort, the Native American faculty envision this course as a shared instructional opportunity that rotates among all of our Native colleagues so that each faculty member is able to teach and contribute their expertise and guidance toward the course learning outcomes.

UNM College of Education Native American Faculty

The UNM COE leads the nation in the number of Native American faculty that represents a diversity of Indigenous peoples. Individually, each faculty member is engaged in research that serves Indigenous peoples and nations. Collectively, Native faculty engage in critical dialogue on issues of scholarship/research, teaching, and service. We acknowledge and operationalize the importance of engaging in research that recognizes the integrity of cultural sovereignty as it is exercised by Indigenous nations. As educators, scholars, and Indigenous peoples, we are cognizant of the critical role that education, Western and Indigenous-centered, has on pedagogy, policy, research, and practice. As such, the COE Native faculty have been committed to working on initiatives with Native American communities and to advance these efforts have collaboratively designed with the support of the COE Dean a major planning grant recently funded by the W. K. Kellogg Foundation (College of Education Institute for American Indian Education Planning Project Phase I). This grant supports COE Native faculty plans to re-establish the Institute for American Indian Education within COE and to engage New Mexico Native nations in examining and identifying future collaboration in three key areas: (a) pre-K–12 impact on school reform, (b) pre-K–20 pathway efforts, and (c) education professional preparation and higher education.

COE Native Faculty Establishing Native-Related Programs

Recognizing the importance of having Native-based and guided programs, the Native American faculty have recently created programs that have been intentional in addressing the needs of New Mexico tribal nations and the education community. For example, the POLLEN (Promoting Our Learning and Leadership and Empowering our Nations) Program, an administrative licensure program for Native American schools in New Mexico, was initiated. In 2017 there were 13 graduates of this program who will go out into the State of New Mexico to increase the number of Native American principals and administrators. The Native American Leadership in Education (NALE) doctoral cohort is another initiative that was created for the purpose of enabling the UNM COE, Teacher Education, Educational Leadership and Policy (TEELP) and the Educational Leadership program to address specific needs within tribes and the broader Native American education community. NALE demonstrates UNM's commitment to Native American nations, as well as Indian education needs in rural and urban communities. The intentional curriculum and program development addresses the unique needs of the communities across the P-20 pipeline while increasing the number of Native American administrators across the education spectrum in New Mexico, nationally and internationally. In the summer 2017, seven Native American doctoral students will have completed their first year and in the fall there will be eight more Native American doctoral students who will join the NALE doctoral cohort. In four to five years, there will be 15 more Native American doctoral recipients in the State of New Mexico with a focus on Indigenous leadership. The Indigenous Research Lab within the Educational Psychology department works with Native American Educational Psychology doctoral students to empower them with research skills so that they are able to contribute this much needed skill in their respective communities or broader education community after completing their doctoral program.

Lastly, the American Indian Language Policy Research and Teacher Training Center engages in a number of sponsored projects that focus on collaborative work with tribal nations engaged in Native language revitalization work. Native graduate students in the COE are mentored and work alongside Native faculty as they develop the skills necessary for respectful working relationships with tribal community members on critical language preservation issues. These examples reflect how Native American faculty members in the College of Education have used their strengths in their respective disciplines and applied their expertise and skillsets to mentoring students, while also contributing to their respective tribal communities, other tribal nations as well as local and national Native-based organizations.

Negotiating MOUs With Native Nations

Another important implication for applying an Indigenous research perspective has recently emerged with the establishment of formal MOUs between the COE and Native nations in New Mexico. These MOUs will encourage reciprocal relationships to be established between Native nations and the College of Education as a means of intentionally addressing the education needs of the community while also ensuring accountability in meeting those needs. We are at the beginning stages of this particular process and will be intentional in our efforts to hold the College of Education accountable in responding to Native nations as a priority. Part of our responsibility as Native researchers, scholars, and members of tribal nations will also be to ensure that these MOUs are created with careful attention to evaluation and assessment processes that involve tribal stakeholders and assure both accountability and effectiveness.

Conclusion

As College of Education Native American faculty and Indigenous scholars, we acknowledge the important role of understanding the historical and contemporary context of New Mexico in relation to Indigenous peoples. We also acknowledge the inherent cultural sovereignty that exists for tribal communities and the political autonomy that this creates. This includes understanding the presence of tribal powers within the framework of sovereignty. All of this informs the research guidelines that should be considered and incorporated when working with Indigenous peoples.

There are numerous implications that stem from this understanding, including the creation of the IERC, the creation of a graduate course addressing Indigenous research paradigms, acknowledging the important role of Native faculty in the College of Education and having Native faculty-led initiatives and programs. Finally, the creation of MOUs with Native nations to strengthen the intentional and continual presence and accountability between them and the UNM College of Education is instructive of the critical work in which we engage as Native scholars and researchers. The UNM College of Education has an opportunity to build on this work and set a precedent in New Mexico as an institution of higher education that values the presence and empowerment of Native faculty and is committed to Native nations in the State of New Mexico. Our hope is that these actions will encourage other institutions of higher education to follow suit.

Robin Zape-tah-hol-ah Minthorn *is a citizen of the Kiowa Tribe of Oklahoma. She is associate professor at the University of New Mexico in Educational Leadership and Native American Studies. Her research interests include Indigenous leadership in higher education, intergenerational Indigenous leadership perspectives, and Native college student experiences.*

Lorenda Belone *is a member of the Navajo Nation and associate professor in the UNM College of Education, Community Health Education Program. For the past 19 years, Dr. Belone has been engaged in community-based participatory research with a focus on health disparities research funded by the National Institutes of Health with Southwest Native American communities.*

Glenabah Martinez *(Taos/Diné) is associate professor in the College of Education at UNM and was raised in Taos Pueblo. Dr. Martinez's research focuses on Indigeneity, youth, and education with an emphasis on Indigenous youth, critical pedagogy, and the politics of social studies curriculum. She captures these research areas in her book,* Native Pride.

Christine Sims *(Acoma Pueblo) is associate professor in the Department of Language, Literacy, and Sociocultural Studies in the UNM College of Education. Dr. Sims' research focuses on issues of American Indian language maintenance and revitalization. She directs the American Indian Language Policy Research and Teacher Training Center.*

REFERENCES

Baldwin, J. A., Johnson, J. L., & Benally, C. C. (2009). Building partnerships between Indigenous communities and universities: Lesson learned in HIV/AIDS and substance abuse prevention research. *American Journal of Public Health, 99*(Suppl. 1), S77–82.

Becenti-Pigman, B., White, K., Bowman, B., Palmanteer-Holder, N. L., & Duran, B. (2008). Research policies, process, and protocol: The Navajo Nation Research Review Board. In M. Minkler & N. Wallerstein (Eds.), *Community-based participatory research for health: From process to outcomes* (2nd ed.) (pp. 441–445). San Francisco, CA: Jossey-Bass.

Belone, L. (2010). An examination of communicative dialectical tensions and paradoxes encountered by Native American researchers in the field and in the academy. Unpublished dissertation, University of New Mexico. World-Cat.org (2010–09–09T21:55:10Z 2010–09–09T21:55: 10Z2010–0909).

Belone, L., Griffith, D. M., & Baquero, B. (2018). Academic positions for faculty of color: combining life calling, community service, and research. In N. Wallerstein, B. Duran, J. Oetzel, & M. Minkler (Eds.), *Community-based participatory research for health: Advancing social and health equity* (3rd ed.) (pp. 265–271). San Francisco, CA: Jossey-Bass.

Belone, L., Oetzel, J. G., Wallerstein, N., Tafoya, G., Rae, R., Rafelito, A., . . . & Thomas, A. (2012). Using participatory research to address substance use in an American-Indian community. In L. R. Frey & K. M. Carragee (Eds.), *Communication activism: Struggling for social justice amidst difference* (vol. 3) (pp. 403–434). New York, NY: Hampton Press, Inc.

Belone, L., Tosa, J., Shendo, K., Toya, A., Straits, K., Tafoya, G., . . . & Wallerstein, N. (2016). Community-based participatory research for co-creating interventions with Native communities: A partnership between the University of New Mexico and the Pueblo of Jemez. In N. Zane, F. Leong, & G. Bernal (Eds.), *Evidence-based psychological practice with ethnic minorities: Culturally informed research and clinical strategies* (pp. 199–220). Washington, DC: American Psychological Association.

Brave Heart, M. Y. H. (2003). The historical trauma response among Natives and its relationship with substance abuse: A Lakota illustration. *Journal of Psychoactive Drugs, 35*(1), 7–13.

Burhansstipanov, L., Christopher, S., & Schumacher, S. A. (2005). Lessons learned from community-based participatory research in Indian Country. *Cancer Control, 12*(Suppl. 12), 70–76.

Christopher, S., Watts, V., McCormick, A. K. H. G., & Young, S. (2008). Building and maintaining trust in a community-based participatory research partnership. *American Journal of Public Health, 98*(8), 1398–1406.

Crump, A. D., Etz, K., Arroyo, J. A., Hemberger, N., & Srinivasan, S. (2017). Accelerating and strengthening Native American health research through a collaborative NIH initiative. *Prevention Science, 4*, 1–4.

Darnton, R. (2003). *George Washington's false teeth: An unconventional guide to the eighteenth century*. New York, NY: W. W. Norton.

Davis, S. M., & Reid, R. (1999). Practicing participatory research in American Indian communities. The *American Journal of Clinical Nutrition, 69*(Suppl.), 755S–759S.

Denetdale, J. (2006). Chairmen, presidents, and princesses: The Navajo Nation, gender, and the politics of tradition. *Wicazo Sa Review, 21*(1), 9–28.

Dickerson, D., Baldwin, J. A., Belcourt, A., Belone, L., Gittelsohn, J., Kaholokula, J. K., . . . & Wallerstein, N. (2018). Encompassing cultural contexts within scientific research methodologies in the development of health promotion interventions. *Prevention Science, 12*, 1–10.

Fisher, P. A., & Ball, T. J. (2005). Balancing empiricism and local cultural knowledge in the design of prevention research. *Journal of Urban Health, 82*(Suppl. 3), 44–55.

Forbes, J. (1994). *Apache, Navajo, and Spaniard*. Norman, OK: University of Oklahoma Press.

Gittelsohn, J., Belcourt, A., Magarati, M., Booth-LaForce, C., Duran, B., Mishra, S. I., . . . & Jernigan, V. B. B. (2018). Building capacity for productive Indigenous community-university partnerships. *Prevention Science, 11*. doi: 10.1007/s11121-018-0949-7

Indian Country Today Media Network (ICTMN Staff). (2012, April 23). President Shelly speaks about Navajo Nation sovereignty day. Retrieved from http://indiancountrytodaymedianetwork.com/2012/04/23/president-shelly-speaks-about-navajo-nation-sovereignty-day-109749.

LaVeaux, D., & Christopher, S. (2009). Contextualizing CBPR: Key principles of CBPR meet the Indigenous research context. *Pimatisiwin: A Journal of Aboriginal and Indigenous Community Health, 7*(1), 1–25.

Lee, L. L. (2010). Navajo transformative scholarship in the twenty-first century. *Wicazo Sa Review, 25*(1), 33–45.

Loewen, J. W. (1999). *Lies across America: What our historic sites get wrong*. New York, NY: The New Press.

Minkler, M., & Wallerstein, N. (Eds.). (2008). Community-based participatory research for health: From process to outcomes (2nd ed.). San Francisco, CA: Jossey-Bass.

NCAI Policy Research Center and MSU Center for Native Health Partnerships. (2012). Walk softly and listen carefully": Building research relationships with tribal communities. Washington, DC, and Bozeman, MT: Authors. Retrieved from http://www.ricai.org/resource/ncai_publications/walk-softly-and-listen-crefully-building-research-relationships-with-tribal-communities.

New Mexico Center on Law and Poverty. (2018). Summary of *Yazzie/Martinez v. State of New Mexico*. Retrieved January 26, 2019 from nmpovertylaw.org/wp-content/uploads/2018/Grapic-Yazzie-Martinez-Decision.pdf.

New Mexico Indian Affairs Department. (2017). *New Mexico's twenty-three tribes and the Indian Affairs Department*. Retrieved from http://www.iad.state.nm.us/history.html.

Nordhaus, R. J., Hall, G. E., & Rudio, A. A. (2003). Revisiting *Merrion v. Jicarilla Apache Tribe*: Robert Nordhaus and sovereign Indian control over natural resources on reservations. *Natural Resources Journal, 43*, 223–284.

Oetzel, J. G. (2009). Intercultural communication: A layered approach. New York, NY: Pearson Education, Inc.

Opler, M. E. (1983). Mescalero Apache. In A. Ortiz (Ed.), *Handbook of North American Indians, Vol. 10: Southwest* (pp. 419–439). Washington, DC: Smithsonian Institution.

Roberts, K. G. (2007). *Alterity and narrative: Stories and the negotiation of western identities*. Albany, NY: State University of New York Press.

Sando, J. (1998). *Pueblo nations: Eight centuries of pueblo Indian history*. Santa Fe, NM: Clear Light Publishers.

Smith, L. T. (2012). *Decolonizing methodologies: research and Indigenous peoples* (2nd ed.). New York, NY: Zed Books.

Straits, K. J. E., Bird, D. M., Tsinajinnie, E., Espinoza, J., Goodkind, J., Spenser, O., Tafoya, N., Willging, C., & the Guiding Principles Workgroup. (2012). *Guiding principles for engaging in research with Native American communities, version 1.* Albuquerque, NM: UNM Center for Rural and Community Behavioral Health and Albuquerque Area Southwest Tribal Epidemiology Center.

Tiller, V. E. (1983). Jicarilla Apache. In A. Ortiz (Ed.), *Handbook of North American Indians, vol. 10: Southwest* (pp. 440–461). Washington, DC: Smithsonian Institution.

Wallerstein, N. B., & Duran, B. (2006). Using community-based participatory research to address health disparities. *Health Promotion Practice, 7*(3), 312.

Wallerstein, N., & Duran, B. (2010). Community-based participatory research contributions to intervention research: the intersection of science and practice to improve health equity. *American Journal of Public Health, 100*(Suppl. 1), S40-S46.

Walters, K. L., & Simoni, J. M. (2009). Decolonizing strategies for mentoring American Indians and Alaska Natives in HIV and mental health research. *American Journal of Public Health, 99*(Suppl. 1), S71-76.

Whitbeck, L. B., Adams, G. W., Hoyt, D. R., & Chen, X. (2004). Conceptualizing and measuring historical trauma among American Indian people. *American Journal of Community Psychology, 33*(3–4). doi: 10.1023/B:AJCP.000 002700.77357.361

Reports From the Field

Pugtallgutkellriit: Developing Researcher Identities in a Participatory Action Research Collaborative

SABINE SIEKMANN, JOAN PARKER WEBSTER,
SALLY ANGASS'AQ SAMSON, CATHERINE
KEGGUTAILNGUQ MOSES, PANIGKAQ AGATHA
JOHN-SHIELDS, AND SHEILA CINGARKAQ WALLACE

Four Alaska Native PhD students and two non-Native university faculty have established a Participatory Action Research (PAR) Collaborative. Our parallel research processes are shaped by and are in turn shaping Western and Indigenous methodologies. We have come to refer to our collaborative as *Pugtallgutkellriit* (those who float together as one), capturing both our epistemology and methodology. Our discussion of positionalities and emergent and dynamic researcher identities draws on recordings and field notes collected while collaborating in various capacities over 11 years.

POSITIONALITIES AND IDENTITIES are dynamic and emerge over time in sociocultural and political contexts. Indigenous teachers are key stakeholders in language revitalization efforts and are uniquely positioned to conduct teacher action research. Yet they face complex challenges as they develop researcher identities. Four Alaska Native PhD students and two non-Native university faculty came together to form a Participatory Action Research (PAR) Collaborative. Drawing on the shared and distinctive positionalities of the collaborators we trace developing individual researcher identities as well as a *collaborative* researcher identity, which is characterized by a dialectic relationship between Western and Indigenous epistemologies.

Because all members of the research collaborative share the goal to support Yup'ik language and culture revitalization, we briefly describe the context of school-based efforts in this area. We then explain the nature of our PAR Collaborative and how the parallel processes we engaged in resulted in a more dynamic and action-oriented model of PAR. Our discussion of positionalities and researcher identities draws on recordings and field notes organized into three phases: (a) teachers as researchers, (b) PhD students as researchers, and (c) Indigenous activist teacher-researchers.

Supporting Yup'ik Language Maintenance and Revitalization Through Graduate Programming and Research

Yup'ik is one of 20 Alaska Native languages (see Figure 1).[1] Krauss (1997) reported that Yup'ik was spoken by approximately 10,000 Yupiit in Southwest Alaska. However, he also noted that children were learning Yup'ik as their first language in only 25% of the communities surveyed. Since that time, language shift to English has continued to disrupt intergenerational transmission of the language.

In order to support language maintenance and revitalization, many communities have established Yup'ik medium instruction (Yup'ik immersion or Yup'ik/English dual language programs) at the elementary school level. Indigenous language immersion programs face many challenges, such as a lack of certified teachers who are highly proficient in the target language and trained in immersion pedagogy; a lack of target language materials in content areas such as science, social studies, and language arts; and a limited number of empirical studies specific to Indigenous language immersion (see, for example, Fortune, Tedick, & Walker, 2008; Iokepa-Guerrero, 2016; Lyster, 2007; Met, 2008; Siekmann, Parker Webster, Samson, & Moses, 2017; Wilson & Kamanā, 2011). The growing body of scholarship points to multiple needs: developing target language proficiency, providing targeted teacher education, creating culturally and linguistically sustaining materials, and improving institutional and political support (Hermes, 2007; Hermes, Cash Cash, Donaghy, Erb, & Penfield, 2016; Lee, 2016; López & García, 2016; Wilson & Kamanā, 2011).

Compared to other Alaska Native languages, Yup'ik immersion programs have historically been relatively well supported. Yup'ik is well documented and substantial written materials are available for teaching and learning the language. Yup'ik language classes are available at the University of Alaska Fairbanks, where students can earn certificates in Yup'ik Language Proficiency and in Native Language Education as

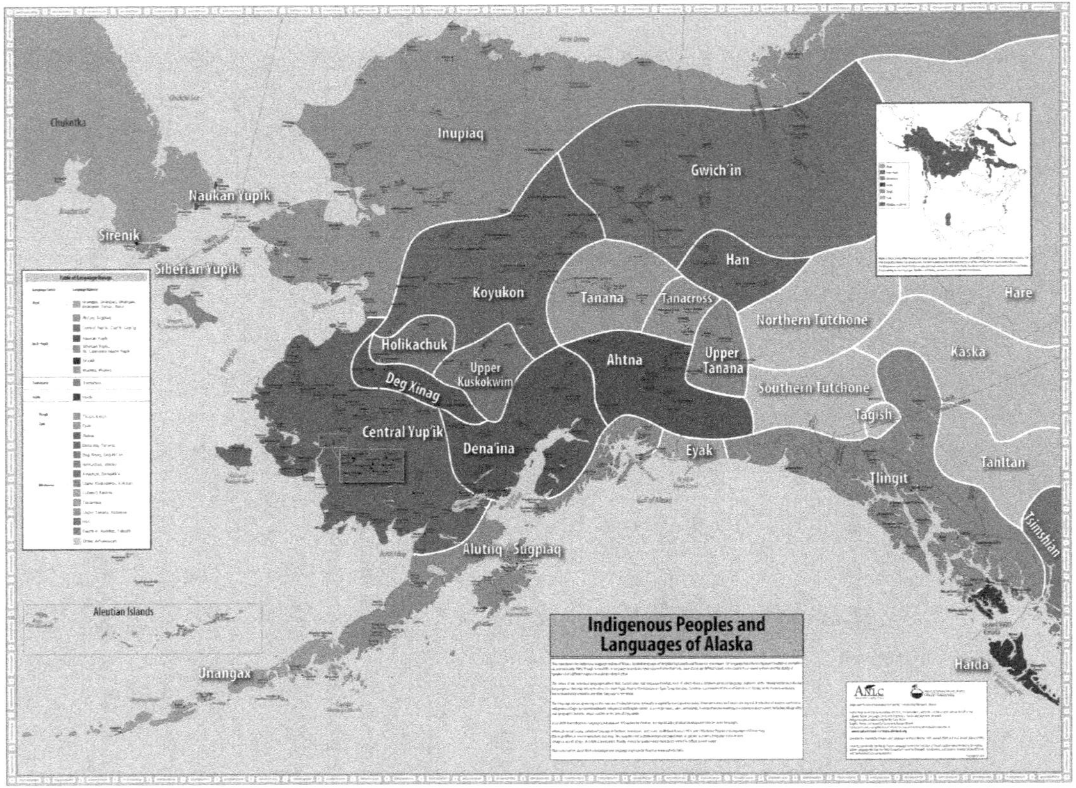

Figure 1. Alaska Native Languages Map. This map depicts the 20 Indigenous languages of Alaska. Central Yup'ik is traditionally spoken in Southwest Alaska. The "Yup'ik" area is approximately the size of the state of Arizona.

well as a BA in Yup'ik Language and Culture. In addition, school districts in Southwest Alaska (particularly the Lower Kuskokwim School District) can draw from a relatively large number of certified teachers who are highly proficient in both spoken and written Yup'ik. Materials development, also, has been ongoing in the local school districts for at least 30 years and at least one of the school districts in Southwest Alaska explicitly supports bilingualism and biliteracy in its mission statement.

However, the need to support Indigenous language maintenance and revitalization efforts through research conducted with and by Indigenous scholars has received insufficient attention in the literature to date. The work we are reporting on here represents one of several parallel initiatives underway in the University of Alaska system, aimed at ameliorating this gap.

The University of Alaska Fairbanks' (UAF) mission statement and core values emphasize its commitment to the circumpolar North and its diverse peoples. UAF's *Strategic Plan 2012–19* proposes to "double the number of Alaska Native graduate students" (University of Alaska Fairbanks, n.d.). In 2009, UAF established a PhD program in Indigenous Studies; since 2008 the university has partnered with the Mellon Foundation to offer dissertation completion fellowships for Alaska Native PhD students. The importance of this work is evident when considering that in 2006, when the coauthors started working together, the University of Alaska had graduated only five Alaska Native PhDs in its history (Alaska Native Knowledge Network, 2013).

Against this backdrop of existing Yup'ik language programs but relatively few Alaska Native PhDs, Sabine and Joan started their collaboration with Yup'ik educators including Sally, Cathy, and Sheila; three regional school districts;[2] an Alaska Native nonprofit organization; and communities in the Yukon Kuskokwim Delta (see Figure 2) located in Southwestern Alaska (Marlow & Siekmann, 2013).

In the following sections, we provide an overview of a series of interlocking grants (see Figure 3), which supported Yup'ik language teaching and locally defined educational research carried out by emergent Indigenous scholars. Our analysis here focuses primarily on the Second Language Acquisition and Teacher Education grant (SLATE), and the Improving Alaska Native Education through Computer Assisted Language Learning grants (ANE CALL), because those projects directly worked to increase the amount of master's and doctoral level research relating to Yup'ik medium instruction.

The SLATE grant supported four Alaska Native PhD students and 18 master's students, all of whom conducted classroom research focusing

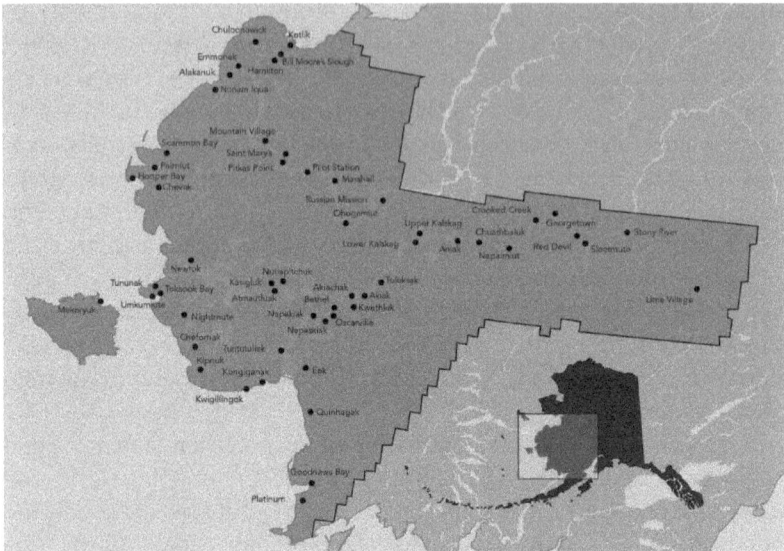

Figure 2. Map of Yukon Kuskokwim Delta Villages. The Yukon Kuskokwim, located in Southwestern Alaska, is home to a number of school districts, including the Lower Kuskokwim School District, the Lower Yukon School District, Kuspuk School, and Yupiit School District. Villages in this region are accessible only by plane, boat, or snow machine, depending on the season. The Lower Kuskokwim School District alone is approximately the size of West Virginia.
(Map courtesy of Calista Education and Culture (2012). Yup'ik Environmental Knowledge Project, map of Yukon-Kuskokwim delta villages, 2012. Boulder, CO: National Snow and Ice Data Center, ELOKA: Exchange for Local Observations and Knowledge of the Arctic. http://eloka-arctic .org/communities/yupik/kuskokwim.html.)

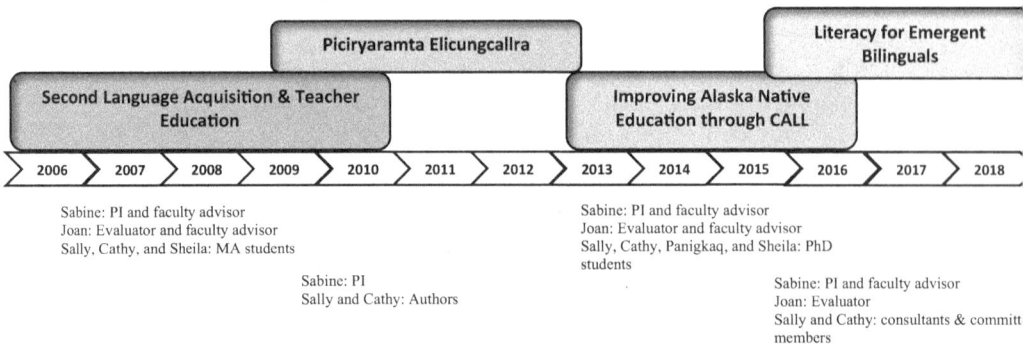

Second Language Acquisition & Teacher Education

Piciryaramta Elicungcallra

Improving Alaska Native Education through CALL

Literacy for Emergent Bilinguals

2006　2007　2008　2009　2010　2011　2012　2013　2014　2015　2016　2017　2018

Sabine: PI and faculty advisor
Joan: Evaluator and faculty advisor
Sally, Cathy, and Sheila: MA students

Sabine: PI
Sally and Cathy: Authors

Sabine: PI and faculty advisor
Joan: Evaluator and faculty advisor
Sally, Cathy, Panigkaq, and Sheila: PhD students

Sabine: PI and faculty advisor
Joan: Evaluator
Sally and Cathy: consultants & committ members

Figure 3. Long-term Collaboration on Grants Supporting Yup'ik Language Teaching through Graduate Programming and Materials Development. This figure provides an overview of a series of interlocking grants on which members of the research collaborative have collaborated in various roles from 2006 to 2018. All projects were funded through the Alaska Native Education Program at the U.S. Department of Education.

on improving Yup'ik and English Language instruction in Southwest Alaska (Marlow & Siekmann, 2012). As a result of this grant, 18 educators from three school districts in the Yukon Kuskokwim Delta earned master's degrees. In addition, four Alaska Native scholars earned a PhD.[3]

The *Piciryaramta Elicungcallra*—Teaching Our Way of Life through Our Language (PE) grant resulted in the publication of 38 Yup'ik medium books for Language Arts instruction in grades K-6 (Siekmann et al., 2013). This project represents the ongoing cyclic nature of teacher action research that was initiated in the SLATE grant in the following two ways: (a) the goals of the PE project were driven by findings generated from the SLATE research, and (b) in order to produce Yup'ik medium books for the language arts curriculum, participating teachers conducted linguistic and cultural research in their communities. Several of the SLATE graduates were part of establishing the grant goals, conducted research in their communities, and authored Yup'ik medium books.

The Improving Alaska Native Education through Computer Assisted Language Learning (ANE CALL) grant supported an additional cohort of four Alaska Native PhD students and additional MA students conducting teacher action research with a focus on technology applications in language teaching. Thirteen MA students (eight focusing on teaching Alaska Native languages, and five focusing on teaching English Language learners) graduated in 2016, and four Alaska Native PhD students are expected to graduate in 2019.

The Literacy for Emergent Bilinguals: Communities of Practice for Teacher Action research supports an additional cohort of 12 master's students. Building on the research trajectory of previous projects, grant-funded teachers are conducting teacher action research in their classrooms to support language and literacy instruction for emergent bilingual students and are expected to graduate in spring 2019.

Pugtallgutkellriit: A Participatory Action Research Collaborative

From 2006 through 2018, a research collaborative emerged through working together on the grant projects described above. The collaborative research group includes four Yup'ik PhD students (Sally, Cathy, Panigkaq, and Sheila) and two non-Native university faculty members (Sabine and Joan). The PhD student members of the collaborative are four Yup'ik women, all highly proficient in their ancestral language (Yugtun) and with many years of experience teaching in Yup'ik medium schools, such as Immersion, Yup'ik First Language, and Dual Language Education. Sally has been a Yup'ik immersion teacher in Bethel for 18 years. Cathy taught in a variety of Yup'ik medium classrooms, most recently in a Yup'ik English Dual Language school in a remote community on the west coast of Alaska. Panigkaq served as a teacher and later as principal for the Yugtun immersion school for 17 years and teaches teacher education courses on multicultural and culturally responsive pedagogy at the University of Alaska Anchorage. Sheila has taught in Yugtun immersion classrooms as well as in secondary Yugtun language classrooms and worked in the Yup'ik curriculum department for the Lower Kuskokwim School District. Joan is a non-Native semi-retired associate professor of Education. As a literacy specialist she has conducted research in the Yup'ik region and has worked with Yup'ik storytellers and educators to create Yup'ik medium texts. Sabine is a German-born applied linguist and language teacher. As a Second Language Acquisition and Language teaching specialist, her primary interests are Alaska Native language teaching and learning, including materials development and computer assisted language learning.

In our research collaborative, we were all engaged in Participatory Action Research (PAR); each PhD student utilized PAR in the research design for her doctoral research. The various grant-related research and program evaluations also utilized PAR. The doctoral student research and the grant-related research thus inform each other, affording opportunities to examine PAR at a meta-level. In addition, we view our research collaborative as an opportunity for dialectic engagements between Western and Indigenous epistemologies and methodologies.

Most authors attribute the foundation of Action Research (AR) to the work of Kurt Lewin (1946), who focused on human dynamics primarily in the workplace (e.g., problems in factory production) and social organizations (e.g., discrimination against minorities). While Lewin was not the first to utilize or advocate the model of AR, he was the first to develop a theory of AR that legitimized it as a systematic and theoretically based form of social science research. AR has developed over the decades and other research approaches, such as PAR, have their roots in AR. AR and PAR have been utilized with Indigenous/Aboriginal peoples in Australia, New Zealand, and Canada focusing on issues of sovereignty, community health, and social justice (see, for example, Herr & Anderson, 2005; Kemmis & McTaggart, 2000). AR is commonly described as a cycle involving planning, acting, observing, and reflecting (Herr & Anderson, 2005). It draws on the 1970s-era work of Paolo Freire, when he created a type of research based on issues of importance to community members—in the case of Freire, literacy issues—and studied these issues collaboratively with the community. In the Freirian-inspired model of participatory research, the academic research model is challenged at almost every point, so that the dualisms of macro/micro, theory/practice, subject/object, and researching/teaching are collapsed.

In our conversations about PAR, methodological discussions about the cyclic nature of the research led us to question the seemingly discrete "steps" of the cycle, especially separating out action as a sometimes "final" step. We talked about how the concept of *upterrlainarluta*, "always getting ready," related to cultural and subsistence activities in Yup'ik culture could be applied to the notion of action in the research cycle. As our students explained: Hunters do not wait until they are ready to go out to hunt to prepare for the action; rather, they are always preparing for the activity, mentally and physically. In other words, action is always taking place in the mind and in physical labor. The actual hunting event is a part of an ongoing cycle of the action of the subsistence activity. Through our discussions of Western and Indigenous epistemology and methodology, we then applied *upterrlainarluta* to the research process. We wondered if action occurs in a more cyclic and recursive fashion, where observing, planning, acting, and reflecting are joined through action. At this point, we co-created our version of the PAR cycle—at each part of the process, there is action: Observing Action, Planning Action, Taking Action, Reflecting on Action (see Figure 4).

Because we are all involved in PAR, we also work together in action-based processes in our roles as advisors and students. In PAR, action is not unidirectional—by that we mean the subject (faculty/Western academic) does not act only on the object (student/Indigenous teachers). Rather, action is characterized by reciprocity and intersubjectivity (subject interacting with subject) through joint collaborative activity (Parker Webster & Siekmann, 2013; Rogoff, Paradise, Arauz, Correa-Chaves, & Angelillio, 2003). Through our parallel processes of PAR, reciprocity and intersubjectivity were put into practice. As methodological tools for analysis, we integrated Indigenous ways of knowing and doing—ontology, epistemology, and methodology—and used Indigenous language. Over the course of our collaboration, we spent many hours talking about the participatory and action-based nature of research and especially how each of us participated in the research collaborative.

As faculty advisors, Joan and Sabine constantly reflected on how to include the doctoral students as collaborative participants in the PAR program evaluation process. One key decision was to include the PhD

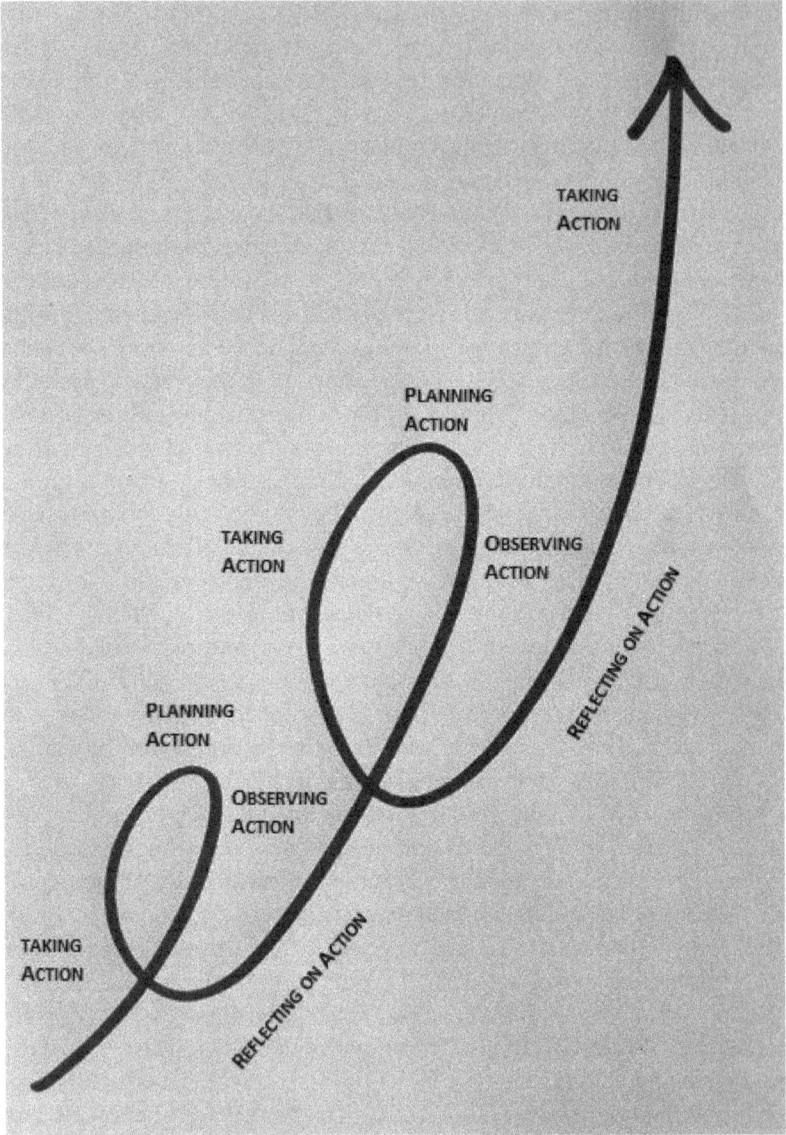

Figure 4. Participatory action research spiral. This figure illustrates how the Pugtallgutkellriit collaborative modified the traditional action research cycle to include action at each step.

students in the analysis of the grant-related PAR data; not only was this a way to put into action the participatory and collaborative nature of PAR, but it was also useful as a pedagogical tool for teaching Western research methods related to PAR. The long-term and intensive engagements with methodological and epistemological concepts undergirding PAR, in our meetings and in research methods classes, prompted discussions about how to conceptualize PAR through a Yup'ik epistemological and methodological stance. From these discussions emerged a new way to talk about collaborative, participatory research that reflected Indigenous/Yup'ik socially organizing principles of doing work together, and *Pugtallgutkellriit* came to be. The term literally means "those who float together as one." It refers to how a subsistence fishing net is held up by a series of floats. To efficiently catch fish, all floats have to be on the same level, floating together. The idea of the same level reflects a Yup'ik value of not putting oneself above others, of collaboratively working together for community well-being (Chief Paul John, personal communication). Re-framing PAR through the Yup'ik concept of collaborative work reciprocally informed and deepened faculty advisors' and doctoral students' understandings of the ethical, theoretical, and methodological underpinnings of PAR. In turn, each student's research project as well as our collaborative grant-related program evaluation research were all enriched.

Developing Researcher Positionalities

Action is a critical aspect of PAR. In order to understand how and why action is carried out by actors in the research process, we must first understand researchers' positionalities and reflexivity. Herr and Anderson (2005) argue, only by "interrogat[ing] our multiple positionalities in relation to the question under study . . . [do] we have the possibility of crafting uniquely complex understandings of the research question. In addition, we hope to avoid the blind spots that come with unexamined beliefs" (p. 44). Being able to examine and think reflexively about our multiple and situated positionalities is key to understanding how and why actions are carried out by researchers and collaborating participants in the research process. Herr and Anderson (2005) offer four ways in which researcher-participants are positioned.

> *Insider/Outsider* positionality vis-à-vis the *setting* under study.
> Hierarchical position or level of informal *power within the organization/ community*.

> Position vis-à-vis dominant groups in society—class, race, ethnicity, gender, sexual orientation, age, ability/disability, religion, and so forth.
> Position within colonial relations within and between nation states.
> (Herr & Anderson 2005, pp. 43–44)

Herr and Anderson's four categories of positionality can be used to interrogate researcher-participant roles and actions in a wide variety of research contexts. In addition, when viewed through the lens of Indigenous researchers researching in and with Indigenous communities, additional layers of ethical, epistemological, and methodological issues emerge (Battiste 2008; Brayboy, 2000; Brayboy & Deyhle, 2000; Smith 1999; Swisher 1998). These issues are particularly salient in the Alaska context, where they are underscored by ethical concerns that are rooted in both historical and very recent accounts of research conducted *on* Alaska Native communities (Deyhle & Swisher, 1997; Lipka, 1998; Parker Webster & John, 2008). Because of research conducted *on* rather than *with* Indigenous peoples, researchers are faced with a history of exploitative research that contributed little to no benefit, or even worse, research that damaged Indigenous peoples and their communities (Parker Webster & John, 2010).

In the case of Indigenous researchers conducting research in Indigenous communities, the tensions between being an Indigenous person and an Indigenous researcher are magnified when viewed against Herr and Anderson's categories (Parker Webster & John, 2010). At this point, we present a (necessarily) partial overview of how we are positioned in our roles as educators and researchers in the context of the research collaborative *Pugtallgutkellriit*.

The doctoral students are Alaska Native teachers in schools serving predominantly Alaska Native students; in that way they are insiders "vis-à-vis the setting under study," while Sabine and Joan, as non-Native university faculty members, are positioned as outsiders. In relation to Western theories and research in the "hierarchical position or level of informal *power within the organization/community*," on the other hand, Joan and Sabine, as tenured university faculty members, are positioned as insiders, while Sally, Cathy, and Sheila were outsiders (at least at the outset of our collaboration). As women, all of us share this gendered *"position vis-à-vis dominant groups in society"* while differences in class, age, religion, family status, and so on distinguish us. We must also acknowledge that our collaborative is made up of Indigenous PhD students working with non-Native faculty members, necessarily positioning us within *"colonial relations"* (Herr & Anderson 2005, pp. 43–44).

We recognize that these positionalities are nested and interrelated; each can be foregrounded or backgrounded at any given time. These nested positionalities are shared by some group members (faculty-faculty, student-student, faculty-student), and shift at various times and within various contexts.

For example, at the beginning of the program, Panigkaq, as a term assistant professor, and Sabine and Joan as tenured associate professors, shared the positionality of university faculty members; Sally, Cathy, and Sheila shared the positionality of K–12 teachers. Presently, Sally's position has shifted, and she is now a tenure-track faculty member at the Kuskokwim Campus in Bethel. Even though we all now share the positionality of university faculty, the asymmetrical power relations that distinctly position senior and junior faculty within this context are still present. Therefore, while we do not feel that naming positionalities such as "woman," "teacher," "faculty," "student," "Native," "non-Native," or "Native speaker" can adequately describe their dynamic complexities, the names do offer a starting point for discussing how actors are positioned in particular contexts.

In the following analysis, we focus on insider-outsider positionalities important to researcher identities that seemed to emerge in three phases in relation to researcher identities: teachers as researchers (during the master's program); student researchers (while in residency at the beginning of the PhD program); activist teacher-researchers (as PhD candidates returning to their communities). In the following sections, we briefly describe the first two time periods, before focusing in more detail on the doctoral students' current research identities.

Teachers as Researchers

Between 2006 and 2010, Sally, Cathy, and Sheila were grant-funded master's students. As part of the SLATE program, each completed a thesis or project in her own classroom. Sally's thesis research integrated *Yuraq* (Yup'ik dance) as a way to teach literacy to immersion kindergarten students. Cathy's thesis research was precipitated by her concern over language shift in the community and focused on teaching an element of Yup'ik grammar in context in a third grade classroom. Sheila's master's project resulted in the creation of a high school Yup'ik class organized around Yup'ik story genres.

Participating in the master's program foregrounded the positionality of teachers who were developing their expertise as immersion educators through coursework (including Second Language Acquisition, Theories and Methods of Second Language Teaching, Materials Development in Second Language Teaching). Engaging in teacher research in their own classrooms positioned them as insiders in relation to their research topics, sites, and participants. The goals of their research grew directly out of needs they had identified in their classrooms, as they worked to improve their own practice. While master's theses are published documents and even though the teachers presented their research at scholarly conferences, at this point in their academic careers the master's students did not view themselves as informing an audience beyond their close colleagues at their site. In other words, while they were conducting research, their teacher positionalities remained foregrounded during the master's program.

As master's level students, as teachers, as Yup'ik women, and as Native speakers of Yup'ik, they remained outsiders to the Western academic research tradition and its discourse. However, during the time in the master's program Sally, Cathy, and Sheila started to develop a new, shared identity. As teachers pursuing master's degrees in a cohort, they read the same literature, completed the same assignments, participated in intensive summer sessions, presented at conferences, and shared the experience of completing a large academic text such as their theses/project.

At the same time, as Sally expresses in the excerpt below, they remained focused on their teacher positionality, and their research stayed contained within their own classrooms.

SALLY: After I completed my masters, I didn't feel like the change happened, because I was by myself in my classroom conducting my research. And I felt like . . . I had this knowledge and I kept it to myself.

PhD Students as Researchers

In 2013, three years after finishing their master's degrees, Sally, Cathy, and Sheila entered the Interdisciplinary PhD program at UAF through funding provided by the ANE CALL grant. At that time, Panigkaq also joined the cohort of Yup'ik PhD students. During the 2013–2014 academic year, all four Indigenous doctoral students left their classrooms, families, and communities to spend time in residency at the main university campus. During this time, they enrolled in 18 credits and completed comprehensive exams. Being on campus as full-time students allowed them to immerse themselves in their studies without the responsibilities of full-time teaching and fostered the development of a learning community of scholars and researchers who grew together and brought together Indigenous and Western ontologies, epistemologies, and methodologies. We identified the residency as a time period when their researcher identities might best be described as PhD students as researchers. During this time, they developed a stronger shared identity as a cohort of emergent Indigenous scholars.

Being in residence foregrounded the "PhD student as researcher" positionality of the cohort of Yup'ik students. As full-time students, Sally, Cathy, Panigkaq, and Sheila took classes on second language teaching and learning, language policy and planning, critical theory, and research methodologies. As they worked toward outsider-insider status in relation to Western academic methodologies, pedagogies, and discourses, the cohort was still positioned as outsiders in relation to the larger campus community. While there were, at times, other Alaska Native master's level students in their classes and even one or two non-Native PhD students, they were the only Alaska Native doctoral students in their shared classes.

Another arena where they shared outsider status involved language use in English and Yup'ik. In their roles as educators, Sally, Cathy, and Sheila used Yup'ik daily with their students, their colleagues, and community members. As doctoral students, they had to use English with their instructors and fellow students, as classes were delivered in English. They grappled not only with the tensions of learning about Western academic theories, but also with the expectations and conventions of academic writing in English.

Contrary to some of the students' home communities, Yup'ik is not widely spoken in the Fairbanks community, which contributed to their outsider positionality. The residency requirement also distanced them from their positionalities as Yup'ik women who have significant responsibilities to family and community. Because of the remoteness of their home communities, they could not go home on weekends, or participate in subsistence and other cultural activities. In part due to this physical distance from families, other colleagues, and community activities, the doctoral students spent significant time with each other beyond the classroom. These times were opportunities to speak Yup'ik, eat Yup'ik food, and participate in traditional activities with Yup'ik friends living in Fairbanks (e.g., taking steam baths); all of these activities contributed to developing shared positionalities as a group of emergent Indigenous scholars.

In addition to completing shared coursework, an important goal of the time in residence was for each PhD student to identify a research agenda and develop their researcher identity. While still relying on their teacher/educator role, they started to view their research as being informed by a broader range of Western and Indigenous theoretical frameworks and as informing a broader audience.

While Cathy's master's research focused on teaching a specific grammatical feature, her dissertation research consists of a year-long investigation of students' language choices and collaboration during a district-mandated instructional strategy. Sally's dissertation research, focused on literacy instruction in the K-6 Yup'ik immersion school, extends her master's research on integrating Yup'ik dance into the teaching of literacy to immersion kindergarten students. As part of her dissertation on culturally responsive teacher education, Panigkaq uses the qasgiq, the traditional Yup'ik educational space, as a metaphor for education that is linguistically and culturally sustaining (John-Shields, 2018). For her MEd, Sheila created a curriculum map for a high school story-based Yup'ik language maintenance class. For her dissertation research, Sheila builds on the high school story-based Yup'ik maintenance class by investigating linguistic and gestural mediation in Yup'ik males during collaborative tasks in her middle school Yup'ik language classroom.

During the residency, the doctoral students began to build shared theoretical and methodological frameworks. As they developed stronger insider positionalities in relation to academic discourse, they began to approach their research from a more critical stance. Questions about insider/outsider positionalities and research identities came to the fore as the cohort brought Indigenous epistemologies and methodologies into conversation with their Western counterparts. The cohort's individual researcher identities and their shared researcher identities began to solidify during the summer session following the year in residence, as they prepared and defended their research proposals and we began to organize our meetings as collaborative writing workshops.

Indigenous Activist Teacher-Researchers

After successfully defending their research proposals and advancing to candidacy, the PhD candidates returned to their communities and resumed their full-time duties as classroom teachers (Sally and Cathy), district office personnel (Sheila), and university faculty (Panigkaq). We continued meeting monthly in the regional hub (Bethel) to provide support during data collection and analysis, and to work on writing their dissertations. During this time, faculty and students developed a strong sense of shared researcher identities, and we named our *Pugtallgutkellriit* collaborative. The Yup'ik cohort began to develop hyphenated positionalities as Indigenous Activist Teacher-Researchers.

As their researcher positionalities and identities strengthened, and they felt increasingly "insiders" within the academy, PhD candidates presented at state, national, and international conferences. Starting in 2015, the newly minted candidates expanded their positionalities from PhD students preparing to do research to Indigenous scholars engaging in research in and for language and cultural revitalization.

As we write, each is enacting different positionalities depending on context: in the academy as researchers and scholars and as Yup'ik women and culture bearers. They continue to negotiate their dynamic, nested, and ever-shifting positionalities in ways that support Yup'ik language and culture maintenance and improve school-based education for Alaska Native students throughout the state of Alaska.

In reflecting on the process of developing Indigenous Activist Teacher-Researcher identities, finding voice, and speaking up emerged as an important theme. Finding voice was closely related to the theme of taking action toward social justice. While each member of our *Pugtallgutkellriit* collaborative experienced this process in their own personal way and we do not intend to homogenize the important particularities of voice and action for each individual, we offer a few examples that reflect key, shared understandings.

Insider/outsider positionalities are dynamic, multifaceted, and complex. Being in the PhD program and conducting research has made their positionalities in their educational institutions more complex, adding not only the outsider status of "being a researcher" but also the lens of critical pedagogy. Negotiating access and permissions for conducting teacher action research in their educational context foregrounded the doctoral candidates' researcher positionalities and thereby the outsider status of researcher rather than the insider status of teacher. Sheila related how principals seemed to feel threatened by the prospect of her conducting doctoral level research in their school.

> SHEILA: I think as Native women, too, here doing research. Cause I sensed it with two principals that I've asked, about the [teaching] positions

available. And once I explained myself and said this is my research and this is what I'm doing, I see that there's a [teaching] position. Is there any way that this can work together? I felt like they were threatened by it. And I'd never seen that part before. It didn't happen to me before. And for it to happen it made me think, wow.

While it is not unusual for Teacher Action researchers to experience push-back and distrust from district and school administrators, the tension between the teacher and researcher positionalities can be amplified for Indigenous and women researchers working in contexts where district personnel and administrators are predominately male and non-Indigenous. Critical pedagogy, with its emphasis on issues of power, access, and representation provided the PhD candidates a lens to recognize how others might feel threatened by their developing positionality as Indigenous Activist Teacher-Researchers.

Navigating the nested and complex positionalities can result in tension with others, and also in inner conflicts, as individuals choose how to position themselves in different contexts. The following examples illustrate the tension between the traditional Yup'ik practice of "being quiet" (insider) and the need to "make noise" (outsider). They illustrate the PhD candidates' move from insider (which they enacted as teachers as researcher) to that of insider-outsiders as Indigenous Activist Teachers-Researchers.

In the following example, Cathy expressed her "inner conflict," illustrating how she enacts her positionalities as both researcher and emerging academic scholar (outsider) in the context of her role as Yup'ik teacher (insider).

> CATHY: And I'm thinking how can we approach this better, how can we— even for Yup'iks. You know, (speaks Yugtun), how we're often quiet, and we let them. . . . It's also part of the status quo we talk about. We either confront them or we let it go and we help things continue as they are without saying anything, while at the same time you have that inner conflict: In Yup'ik way you don't do this, you don't stand up and make noise, like they say.

Cathy explains how her complicated positionalities led her to question how she could enact a more activist role in contexts such as staff meetings. Her engagement with Western theory, including critical pedagogy, allowed her to articulate questions about power and hegemonic practices.

CATHY: You think, why am I doing this? And how can I improve on that? At the same time during staff meetings, things I read about, like the hegemony thing, those are playing in the back of my mind.

Panigkaq describes how writing in her researcher journal made her more aware of her insider and outsider positionality. This, in turn, prompted her to take a more critical stance at the intersection of teaching and researching.

PANIGKAQ: Or I'll say I'm starting to use my researcher journal position as I'm teaching. I'm starting to question a lot more . . . I had to think of my insider and outsider position. And I mentioned how I was more aware of my researcher self rather than keeping myself as an educator.

While positionalities can sometimes be in conflict, the resultant tensions can also be negotiated in ways that support language and culture maintenance. While Sally experiences conflicting positionalities, she is starting to negotiate when and how to foreground and background each positionality. Rather than feeling like she has to enact one positionality over another at all times, she is "waking up" to the notion that these are constantly in negotiation and she can actively evaluate which to enact at which time.

SALLY: There are times we can sit and be quiet and listen, there are times when we have to speak up. To make changes. So that's . . . I feel like I'm in conflict. And waking up at the same time.

Recognizing one's dynamic, nested, and complex positionalities enhances the ability to reflexively question who benefits from an action. As Indigenous Activist Teacher-Researchers, members of the *Pugtallgutkellriit* collaborative continually find themselves in liminal spaces where teaching and researching as well as insider and outsider positionalities meet.

Conclusion: Working the Hyphen

Fine (1994) uses the phrase "working the hyphens" to describe working across cultures. For Fine, the hyphen occupies an intensely complex space, the gap within the Indigene-colonizer relationship, and it evokes our shared past, bringing to the forefront the name of each—the Indigene and colonizer are each produced by the other. The hyphen is a marker of the relationship between collaborating peoples as well as their respective relationship to difference.

Similarly, the hyphen can also be used to explain the complicated relationship between teacher-researcher in the Teacher Action Research (TAR) approach. Like Indigene-colonizer, each positionality—of teacher and researcher—is produced by the other. The production occurs in the day-to-day pedagogy that reflects theory (researcher) and practice (teacher); reflecting the Freirean (Freire, 1977) notion of how "theory into practice" and "practice into theory" are each sides of the same coin, coexisting together. In TAR, both teacher and researcher exist in a complex relationship that springs from praxis, where the teacher and the researcher positionalities must act together upon the social environment in order to critically reflect upon reality and so transform it through further action and critical reflection.

Sabine Siekmann *is associate professor of linguistics and foreign languages at the University of Alaska Fairbanks. She is an applied linguist and language teacher committed to improving the education of bilingual and biliterate children. Her research interests include computer assisted language learning (CALL), teaching language through story and task-based approaches, and applications of sociocultural theory in language teaching and learning.*

Joan Parker Webster *is retired associate professor of education at the University of Alaska Fairbanks (UAF). Currently affiliated faculty in the Center for Cross Cultural Studies at UAF and evaluator for federally funded grant programs, she also conducts ethnographic research in Alaska Native communities and publishes in the areas of multiliteracies, multimodal analysis, research methodologies, and Indigenous education.*

Sally Angass'aq Samson *is assistant professor of Yup'ik language and culture at Kuskokwim Campus in Bethel, Alaska. Prior to that, Sally taught for 19 years at the Ayaprun Elitnaurvik Immersion Charter School. She earned a master's degree in applied linguistics in 2010 from the University of Alaska Fairbanks and is currently pursuing her PhD.*

Catherine Keggutailnguq Moses *is a retired elementary teacher of Lower Kuskokwim School District. She was born and raised in Kotlik, Alaska; married into the community of Toksook Bay, Alaska; and is currently working on her dissertation through the University of Alaska Fairbanks.*

Panigkaq Agatha John-Shields *is term assistant professor of School of Education at University of Alaska Anchorage (UAA). She is affiliated with Indigenous Education and teaching and currently teaches in undergraduate and graduate levels throughout the different education programs.*

Sheila Cingarkaq Wallace *is curriculum specialist-Yup'ik at the Lower Kuskokwim School District in Bethel, Alaska. Currently she develops secondary Yup'ik curriculum and teaches Yup'ik for high school students in surrounding villages through video-conferencing. She is pursuing her PhD in applied linguistics at the University of Alaska Fairbanks with a focus on second language acquisition in Yup'ik context.*

NOTES

1. Nineteen of these languages are actively spoken in Alaska. The last fluent speaker of Eyak passed away in 2008, and the Eyak language is now considered to be dormant.

2. Lower Kuskokwim School District, Lower Yukon School District, Kuspuk School District.

3. After three years of funding through the SLATE grant, all PhD candidates were successful in applying for the Andrew W. Mellon Foundation Dissertation Fellowship, which was created for Alaska Native and Pacific Islander scholars and others committed to the advancement of Indigenous Alaskan and Pacific Islander history and culture. https://www.uaf.edu/gradsch/grants-and-fellowships/mellon/index.xml. Walkie Charles, April Laktonen Counceller, and Hishinlai' Peter earned PhDs with an emphasis on Applied Linguistics within the Interdisciplinary PhD program, and Theresa Arevgaq John earned a PhD in Indigenous Studies. Hishinlai' Peter is expected to graduate in spring 2019.

REFERENCES

Alaska Native Knowledge Network. (2013, August 1). Alaska Native men and women with earned research doctorates. Retrieved from http://ankn.uaf.edu /Curriculum/PhD_Projects/AKNativePhDs.html.

Battiste, M. (2008). Research ethics for protecting indigenous knowledge and heritage: Institutional and research responsibilities. In N. K. Denzin & Y. S. Lincoln (Eds.), *Handbook of critical and Indigenous methodologies* (pp. 497–509). Los Angeles, CA: SAGE.

Brayboy, B. M. J. (2000). The Indian and the researcher: Tales from the field. *International Journal of Qualitative Studies in Education, 13,* 415–426.

Brayboy, B. M. J., & Deyhle, D. (2000). Insider-outsider: Researchers in American Indian communities. *Theory Into Practice, 39* (3), 163–168.

Calista Education and Culture (2012). Yup'ik environmental knowledge project: Map of Yukon-Kuskokwim delta villages. Boulder, CO: National Snow and Ice Data Center, ELOKA: Exchange for Local Observations and Knowledge of the Arctic. Retrieved online http://eloka-arctic.org/communities /yupik/kuskokwim.html [01/20/2019].

Deyhle, D., & Swisher, K. (1997). Research in American Indian and Alaskan Native education: From assimilation to self-determination. *Review of Research in Education, 22*, 113–94.

Fine, M. (1994). Working the hyphens: Reinventing self and other in qualitative research. In N. K. Denzin & Y. S. Lincoln (Eds.), *Handbook of qualitative research* (pp. 70–82). Thousand Oaks, CA: SAGE.

Freire, P. (1977). *Cultural action for freedom.* London, UK: Penguin.

Fortune, T. W., Tedick, D. J., & Walker, C. L. (2008). Integrated language and content teaching: Insights from the immersion classroom. In T. W. Fortune & D. J. Tedick (Eds.), *Pathways to multilingualism: Evolving perspectives on immersion education* (pp. 71–96). Clevedon, UK: Multilingual Matters, Ltd.

Hermes, M. (2007). Moving towards the language: Reflections on teaching in an Indigenous-immersion school. *Journal of American Indian Education, 43*(3), 54–71.

Hermes, M., Cash Cash, P., Donaghy, K., Erb, J., & Penfield, S. (2016). New domains for Indigenous language acquisition and use in the USA and Canada. In S. M. Coronel-Molina & T. L. McCarty (Eds.), *Indigenous language revitalization in the Americas* (pp. 269–291). New York, NY: Routledge.

Herr, K., & Anderson, G. L. (2005). *The action research dissertation.* Thousand Oaks, CA: SAGE.

Iokepa-Guerrero, N. (2016). Revitalization programs and impacts in the USA and Canada. In S. M. Coronel-Molina & T. McCarty (Eds.), *Indigenous language revitalization in the Americas* (pp. 227–246). New York, NY: Routledge.

John-Shields, A. (2018). *Tangerqengiaraucaraq (Being Present).* PhD dissertation, University of Alaska Fairbanks.

Kemmis, S., & McTaggart, R. (2000). Participatory action research. In N. K. Denzin & Y. S. Lincoln (Eds.), *Handbook of qualitative research* (pp. 567–605). Thousand Oaks, CA: SAGE.

Krauss, M. (1997). Indigenous languages of the North: A report on their present state. In. H. Shoji & J. Janhunen (Eds.), *Northern minority languages: Problems of survival. Senri Ethnological Studies, 44*, 1–34. Osaka, Japan: National Museum of Ethnology.

Krauss, M., Holton, G., Kerr, J., & West, C. T. (2011). Indigenous peoples and languages of Alaska. Fairbanks and Anchorage: Alaska Native Language Center and UAA Institute of Social and Economic Research. Retrieved from http://www.uaf.edu/anla/map.

Lee, T. S. (2016). The home-school-community interface in language revitalization in the USA and Canada. In S. M. Coronel-Molina & T. L. McCarty (Eds.), *Indigenous language revitalization in the Americas* (pp. 99–115). New York, NY: Routledge.

Lewin, K. (1946). Action research and minority problems. *Journal of Social Issues, 2* (4), 34–46.

Lipka, J., with Mohatt, G. V., and the Ciulistet Group. (1998). *Transforming the culture of schools: Yup'ik Eskimo examples.* Mahwah, NJ: Lawrence Erlbaum.

López, L., & García, F. (2016). The home-school-community interface in language revitalization in Latin America and the Caribbean. In S. M. Coronel-Molina & T.L. McCarty (Eds.), *Indigenous language revitalization in the Americas* (pp. 116–135). New York, NY: Routledge.

Lyster, R. (2007). *Learning and teaching languages through content: A counterbalanced approach*. Philadelphia, PA: John Benjamins.

Marlow, P., & Siekmann, S. (2012). Changing the conversation: Promise and vulnerability in Alaska Native language revitalization. *Journal of American Indian Education, 51*(3), 46–69.

Marlow, P., & Siekmann, S. (Eds.) (2013). *Communities of practice: An Alaska native model for language teaching and learning*. Tucson, AZ: University of Arizona Press.

Met, M. (2008). Paying attention to language: Literacy, language and academic achievement. In T. W. Fortune & D. J. Tedick (Eds.), *Pathways to multilingualism: Evolving perspectives on immersion education* (pp. 49–70). Clevedon, UK: Multilingual Matters.

Parker Webster, J., & John, T. (2008). Exploring parallel ways of knowing and expressing knowledge: Yup'ik music, dance and oral storytelling. Paper presented at the Annual Forum on Ethnography and Education, February 18–22, Philadelphia, PA.

Parker Webster, J., & John, T. (2010). Preserving a space for cross-cultural collaborations: an account of insider/outsider issues. *Ethnography and Education, 5*(2), 175–291.

Parker Webster J., & Siekmann, S. (2013). Mentoring: Engaging communities of practice. In P. Marlow, & S. Siekmann (Eds.), *Communities of practice: An Alaska Native model for language teaching and learning* (pp. 46–76). Tucson, AZ: University of Arizona Press.

Rogoff, B., Paradise, R., Arauz, R. M., Correa-Chavez, M., & Angelillio, C. (2003). First hand learning through intent participation. *Annual Review of Psychology, 54*, 175–203.

Siekmann, S., Parker Webster, J., Samson, S., & Moses, C. (2017). Teaching our way of life through our language: Materials development for Indigenous immersion education. *Cogent Education, 4*, 1362887. https://doi.org/10.1080/233 1186X.2017.1362887.

Siekmann, S., Thorne, S., John, T., Andrew, B., Nicolai, M., Moses, C., Lincoln, R., Outon, C., Samson, S., Westlake, J., Miller, G., Winkelman, V., Nicholai, R., & Bass, S. (2013). Supporting Yup'ik medium education: Progress and challenges in a university-school collaboration. In S. May (Ed.), *LED2011: Refereed conference proceedings of the 3rd International Conference on Language, Education and Diversity* (pp. 1–25). Auckland, NZ: The University of Auckland.

Smith, L. T. (1999). *Decolonizing methodologies: Research and Indigenous peoples*. London, UK: Zed Books.

Swisher, K. (1998). Why Indian people should be the ones to write about Indian education. In D. A. Mihesuah (Ed.), *Natives and academics: Researching and writing about American Indians* (pp.190–199). Lincoln, NE: University of Nebraska Press.

University of Alaska Fairbanks. (n.d.). Strategic plan. Retrieved from https://www.uaf.edu/strategic/2012/.

Wilson, W. H, & Kamanā, K. (2011).Insights from Indigenous language immersion in Hawai'i. In D. Tedick, D. Christian, & T. Williams Fortuen (Eds.), *Immersion education: Practices, policies, possibilities* (pp. 36–57). Bristol, UK: Multilingual Matters.

Contributor Information

The *Journal of American Indian Education* (*JAIE*) is a refereed journal publishing original scholarship about education issues of American Indians, Alaska Natives, Native Hawaiians, and Indigenous peoples worldwide, including First Nations, Māori, Aboriginal/Torres Strait Islander peoples, Indigenous peoples of Latin America, Africa, and others. *JAIE* strives to improve Indigenous education through empirical research; knowledge generation; and transmission to researchers, communities, and diverse educational settings.

JAIE encourages dialogues among researchers and practitioners through research-based articles elucidating current educational issues and innovations. *JAIE* also invites original scholarly essays advancing a point of view about an educational question or issue, when supported by cited research literature; original reviews of literature in underexplored areas; original expository manuscripts that develop or interpret a theory or issue; and Reports From the Field. Studies grounded in Indigenous research methodologies are especially encouraged.

Prepare manuscripts according to the most recent *Publication Manual of the American Psychological Association* (6th ed.) (http://www.apastyle.org/manual/index.aspx). Format manuscripts in Microsoft Word and blind for anonymous peer review; manuscripts not blinded or appropriately formatted will be returned. Authors must certify that the manuscript is not being considered by another publisher. All empirical studies must document: (1) the use of accepted ethical protocols for research with human subjects; and (2) site-specific approvals, including research and/or institutional review board approvals required by Native nations, tribes, or bands as well as schools and school districts, where appropriate. Please use the term most appropriate to the Indigenous group or people to whom the manuscript refers. *American Indian/Alaska Native, Native American, Native Hawaiian,* and *Indigenous* are acceptable terms when referring to Indigenous peoples of the United States. *JAIE* reviews only one manuscript at a time from an author (or co-author). If a manuscript is under review, the Editorial Team cannot accept another manuscript (either single authored or co-authored) until the first manuscript clears the review process.

All manuscripts must be submitted electronically to jaie@asu.edu. Submit: (1) double-spaced manuscript as one Word document (do not send a pdf), including the title and abstract (maximum 150 words); (2) biographical statement(s) for each author (50 words each), and contact information for each author, including author name, affiliation, email address, physical street address; and phone number. Do not include author name(s) on or in the manuscript.

Feature-length Manuscripts. Original scholarly manuscripts should be double-spaced, 7,500–8,000 words total, including endnotes, if any, and references.

Reports From the Field. Original scholarly manuscripts providing descriptive, evaluative, and/or policy-oriented analyses of innovative education models and practices. Reports should be up to 5,000 words, including endnotes, if any, and references. See the website and *JAIE* 49(3) for a fuller description of *RFTF.*

Indigenous Policy Forum. Invited manuscripts. The *IPF* functions as a current conversational space and as important historical archive, featuring the voices and vision of Indigenous education policymakers, policy implementers, and activists.

Manuscripts will be considered throughout the year and, if accepted, will be published in any of the three issues at the direction of the editorial staff. There is no remuneration for *JAIE* contributors; authors will receive two free copies of the issue in which the manuscript is published. For more information see the *JAIE* website at http://jaie.asu.edu.

JOURNAL OF AMERICAN INDIAN EDUCATION

CALL FOR PEER REVIEWERS

AS A PEER-REVIEWED JOURNAL, *JAIE* depends upon the generosity of our colleagues in the field of Indigenous education. Rigorous, constructive, and supportive peer review is essential to the health of our field and to the quality of our journal.

We invite interested academic colleagues, practitioners, and advanced doctoral students to sign up as peer reviewers for *JAIE*. Your name will be added to the database we consult for reviews of submitted manuscripts. *JAIE* uses double-blinded peer review: the identities of manuscript authors are not shared with reviewers, and the identities of peer reviewers are not shared with authors. If you are already a reviewer for the journal, please log on to the new website and fill out a Reviewer Application so we have updated information in our database.

The responsibilities of peer review include:

- Timely response to requests to review, letting the editorial assistant know if you can review the submitted manuscript

- Completion of review within three to four weeks of receiving the manuscript

- Detailed commentary on the strengths and weaknesses of the manuscript, including its contribution to knowledge, adherence to ethical standards of research, narrative and organizational coherence, and relevance of analytic or descriptive content

- Constructive and supportive suggestions to improve or enhance the manuscript.

To sign up, please visit the *JAIE* website at https://jaie.asu.edu/. At the foot of the home page, click on Reviewer Application. Fill out the fields of the online form, attach a PDF copy of your c.v., and click Submit.

Thank you!